Ruby's Harmonicas & Pianos, Incorporated

A Play in Three Acts

By Gregory Powell

Ruby's Harmonicas & Pianos, Incorporated

A Play in Three Acts

Graphic design: "Reclining II" Linda LeKinff. Acrylic on wood ©2006

ISBN 10: 1-938373-12-X
ISBN 13: 978-1-938373-12-1
Library of Congress Control Number: 2019936860

Printed in the United States of American by KDP

Lanham MD

[illegible]

Printed in the United States of America [illegible]

Table of Contents

Foreword

The poet Nikki Giovanni once said, "Histories are important because they point us toward the direction of our traditions." I was introduced to playwright and poet, Gregory Powell, a graduate of Morehouse College in the tradition of our "Morehouse Brotherhood" through our dear friend and colleague Broadway artist, Russell Joel Brown (The Lion King). After bearing witness to Mr. Powell's thought provoking and engaging poetry book, Tin Ears, I was given the opportunity to read his very first play, Ruby's Harmonicas & Pianos Incorporated. Mr. Powell's fictional history telling play is a testimony to various traditions we inherit from America's family remembrances by looking back at our past, embracing our present; and moving forward to our future.

Mr. Powell's dramatic play (with a flare of comedic timing) touches on themes of slavery, immigration, civil rights (Bloody Sunday), education, unions and stolen "black vs white" family legacies. The play is set in the deep south in the summer of 1969 in Memphis, Tennessee in the United States of America – one year after the assassination of Dr. Martin Luther King Jr., and the height of the Vietnam War.

Mr. Powell who worked several years as a news reporter for the Memphis Business Journal utilizes his reporting skills to craft a new American play that is timely for our trans-media ready global generation. The story telling "is pregnant with expectation and the water is about to break." (a line uttered by a main character as the play unravels). Ironically, the publication of Mr. Powell's newly developed first play marks the 65th anniversary of the Brown vs The Board of

Education of Topeka, Kansas –the landmark United States Supreme Court case in which the Court declared state laws establishing separate public schools for black and white students to be unconstitutional.

And the tradition continues. And so it is. And so it shall be.

Charles Reese, *Actor/Author/ Cultural Architect for Public Engagement*
The James Baldwin Literary & Conversation Salon Series
Los Angeles, CA

Preface

Manna and The Blues

I think I'm drownin' on dry land."
- Little Junior Parker

Recently my sister Tricia rediscovered the song (Little Junior Parker's "Drowning on Dry Land") that our dad (Franklin Powell, a/k/a "Red") repeatedly played on the turntable of our stereo. He had played Parker's 45 so many times that the needle on our stereo slowly gnawed every groove on the record, until the vinyl was as smooth as one of my mother's plates. No problem – dad would gas up our Buick, drive to Pop Tunes on Summer Avenue (Memphis) and buy another wafer-thin 45. My siblings and I had memorized the words of the song, often singing along with Parker and my dad as Parker was spinning on our turntable.

Of course, at that point, we could not appreciate the satire threading through Parker's chorus, "Sometimes I feel like I am drowning on dry land." How can a man drown on dry land where there is no water? (If you are not a swimmer, land is a safe place to be, right?) We loved, instead, that dad was enraptured by Parker's lyrics, and that he loved blues more than bread; today, we love the same blue bread. We loved the rhythm of the song and other bluesmen and blues women; we loved that the words drew us into a familial circle of love and faith and oneness - as dad drove our Buick along the back roads leading to/from Memphis, with the windows down, WDIA (FM) blaring every one of Little Junior Parker's sins, if you cared to listen to his testimony across WDIA's airwaves; Parker and other musicians like BB

King confessed like the saints at church, dropping his head so that he could lift it again and again. What is the Blues? Blues is living and surviving and thriving on what would kill someone else…someone without hope. That began my love for words and how blues and language can feed the human soul. I was enraptured. Then, once I learned to read, I fell in love with the Psalms. In Psalm 6:6, David laments, "I am tired of crying to you (God); every night my bed is wet with tears." I saw a connection between the lament of Little Junior Parker (Memphis, Tennessee) and King David (Israel).

Then, I wondered if Little Junior Parker and King David were brothers in blues and bone, because both men knew how to employ language that welcomed us into the marrow of life and love, loss, fullness, hate and seamless hope, fear, blessedness and corruption, redemption and reconciliation? Had the two men, Little Junior Parker and King David, eaten from the same dented, tin plate – anointed by their pain, promise and hope? Leadbelly had eaten from the same tin plate, but he'd grown stronger with each plateful he'd gulped behind the walls of Parchman Prison. Surely, these three men had sipped sweet water from the same wide-mouth Mason jar. Had they lived next-door to one another on Beale Street in Memphis, where raw life spilled onto the streets, framing every front porch in this city of blues and want with hope? Maybe they had borrowed the occasional cup of sugar from one another, between paychecks, as neighbors do down south? I was enraptured by their language and its monolithic possibilities to redeem, reconcile, change, record, and spread victory for humankind.

As a teenager, I started writing poems (thank you, Mrs. Gwendolyn Brooks, rest in peace), incomplete plays, short stories and very unsuccessful essays, and reflected about Little Junior Parker, my mom (Florence Williams Powell), Thurgood Marshall, B. B. King, my dad, Ella Fitzgerald, blues ethics, Bessie Smith, King David, Paul Dunbar, narrative and haiku, Tampa Red, King Solomon, satire, Miles Davis, Harriet Tubman, Lot's wife who had turned into a pillar of salt, Coltrane and his bad brass ax, Mahalia Jackson, and my pastor's sermons (Reverend Wiley Harris). These people had turned up the lights on the lives, politics, challenges, strength and economic challenges of African Americans and other people of color who were living, suffering, hoping, fighting and thriving in the iron footnote of American Society. Yes, these people were drowning on dry land. Likewise, the fictional characters in "Ruby's Harmonicas & Pianos, Incorporated," were drowning on dry land, but, thanks to God, they're learning to swim…on dry land.

Gregory Powell

1 April 2019

Characters

Remmy – black male, late 40s.

Will – black male, late 40s.

Bryan DuBose (aka Radio) – black male, late 50s. Because of the last scene in the play, where Radio bares his back so the audience can see a "Tree of Scars" on his back, it is important for Radio to be as light-skinned as possible. Radio is tall, broad-shouldered, very imposing. Radio represents Truth in the play, and truth is always bold and uncompromising.

Floyd Holiday – white male, late 20s, very arrogant and condescending. The actor who plays Floyd in the play will also play the Memphis Banker.

Memphis Banker – White male, no name, early 60s; Floyd plays the banker to emphasize that racism, white religious lethargy and ignorance can leach from one generation to the next. The Banker represents institutional racism in corporate America.

Catherine – black female, late 20s; she is nine-months pregnant at beginning of play.

Rueben Holstein (a/k/a Franklin Rubine Holiday) – white male, early 20s; appears only in two flashback scenes.

Ruby Holiday – black female, early 20s, appears only in one flashback.

Setting

The play takes in Memphis, Tennessee, August, 1969. Most of the scenes are set either at a Church or in Floyd's office at Ruby's Harmonicas & Pianos, Incorporated; however, the first flashback scene is staged with only several small tables, upon which blueprints, etc., are spread, and the second flashback scene is set in the office of the Memphis Banker (sparsely furnished with a desk and one armchair). Race relations, institutional racism, union organizational drives, and economic segregation are at a boiling point in Memphis and throughout the south.

Act 1 Scene 1

(The light comes up inside the church: There are about five rows of chairs with six chairs in each row. The backs of these chairs face the audience, giving the audience the impression that they are part of the Cast; hopefully they will become emotionally vested in the play early on. Will stands behind a small lectern, presiding over the meeting of employees from Ruby's Harmonicas and Pianos. Remmy sits in chair to Will's right and Catherine sits in a chair to his left. There is a small table next to Remmy and there is a rotary telephone on the table. Radio is seated with his coworkers and he holds his composure throughout the scene, although everyone else asks questions and laughs and talks. The cast should be wearing buttons that read "Vote Union," and there should be a few large signs which read "Vote Union."

Will:

(*Employees raise their hands and Will begins to patiently answer their questions and address their concerns. Some of the employees are not completely sold on the union, and some fear they will be terminated if the company discovers they are supporting the Union. Although Will is not a preacher, he "preaches" here with vigor to both encourage and embolden his coworkers*). We have three shifts at Ruby's Harmonicas and Pianos; most of us work different shifts. I don't know all your names – not yet. I know you have a lot of questions. I can understand your worry and fear. But before we get started I want to thank you for voting me, Remmy (*standing, raising his hand, and reclaiming his seat)* and Catherine (*stands and calmly places her hands on stomach and then retains her seat; she is nine-months pregnant)* as your union representatives for Harmonicas &

Pianos Makers Union. From the beginning people said we couldn't do it. Or don't do it. Or why you doing it? I say we wanna be treated fairly; want better wages; better working conditions. Who are the two foot-soldiers behind me? *(looking at Remmy)* - I've known him all my life. Remmy is a lion. Amen (*then, chorus of "Amens" ripple on the stage by the Cast)*. He is as committed as he is courageous. Nothing gets pass Remmy. And Catherine is a Tigress, who is as wise as an owl. *(He looks at Catherine)* As you can see, she's *tumbling big*. Let's pray she can vote tomorrow before her baby comes roaring into the light. Amen?

Another fact you need to know about her: she's the only woman to ever work the production line; there's not a man on her shift who can out-work her, black or white. Amen. (*another chorus of "Amens" ripple through the Cast)*. Before I answer your questions, I want to thank you for your prayers. *(Will begins his sermon)* Keep praying. First, I have a few comments about the local newspapers; the media is not the friend of rank-and-file employees. Heaven forbid the newspapers be objective; not one reporter has ever interviewed me; never asked why we organizing Ruby's. Take the *Memphis Business Daily News,* for instance. This morning, I read an editorial titled "Children of Judas." (*Will is still preaching)* This editor compares you and I to the man who betrayed Jesus Christ. I'm honored to be held in such high esteem. Especially a newspaper that prints a full-page ad supporting Ruby's anti-union position; the paper considers the "free" ad a public service announcement. That means Ruby's don't pay a dime for the ad. It's not a PSA if the Union is never given the opportunity to voice its position, relative to hours, wages, and conditions of employment. Where is the Union's free ad? Amen? *(There is a chorus of 'Amens' from the Cast).* Brothers and Sisters, what I found most troubling about the editorial this morning was the editor's position. He writes, "Now is not the time to organize Ruby's." It's easy to say, "Now Is Not The Time" if you're making all the money; if you have the best benefits; if you're given special treatment." (*Will reaches the epicenter of his Sermon, and the Cast responds as if it's Sunday morning; a few of them stand; a few lift their hands)* If this newspaper was worth its salt, at least one reporter could have contacted me, or Remmy or Catherine. Let us explain how we feel, earning twenty-seven percent less a hour than our white brothers and sisters. We perform the same job; some of us have twice the seniority. (*pounding the lectern with his fist)* Now "is" the best time to organize Ruby's. The same job should equal the same pay; don't matter your race or your sex.

Catherine:

We want better benefits –

Remmy:

Better working conditions – More respect.

Will:

Some of our white brothers and sisters receive more sick days and personal days. Now, let's answer your questions. Your name, Brother?

Sam:

May name is Sam. When you count the employees on all three shifts at Ruby's, we have about two-hundred-and-fifty to three-hundred men and women. Roughly forty five percent of those are white employees (*Sam looks at the Cast*). There's not one white person here tonight-

Man from the Cast:

White folk don't go to black churches, unless it's a funeral or we baptizing. Everybody should know that.

Woman from the Cast:

True. True. But, let's move on.

Catherine:

Our bargaining unit is composed of three- hundred-and-twenty voters.

Sam:

Not all black people at Ruby's gonna vote for the Union; some of us won't sign a union card, which simply says you support it. How are the white folk gonna vote tomorrow? If it's a tight vote, we'll need some white folk to vote union too.

Woman from Cast:

I invited Phil Jenkins and he told me no white man in his family had never set one foot in a black church. And he was not about to break family tradition.

Will:

Thank God not all our white coworkers think like Phil; some of them have supported us since day one. But they don't want Ruby's to know; some signed union cards; some asked me for union cards. We have to trust they have our backs. When we filed our Petition for an Election with the Labor Board we turned in just enough cards. Just barely enough.

Sam:

Does it mean thirty percent will vote for the union tomorrow? Even if you signed a card you have to vote union when they hand you that ballot. And we need one vote over fifty percent for the union to wrap this thing up.

Remmy:

You're right, Sam, but I've talked to a lot of our white sisters and they've given me their word they will vote union tomorrow; some have even signed union cards. Now, I can't say how a majority of the white men will vote. I got a lot of their women to support us, but they gotta keep it quiet. Can't walk around the plant wearing buttons that say, "Vote Union."

Sam:

We don't know if they'll vote for Ruby's or the Union tomorrow. After the Board Agent hands them a ballot, they could check "No" for the Union and "Yes" for Ruby's.

Will:

Sam, listen to Remmy because he knows what he's talking about.

Catherine:

Some white women love the Brothers, behind closed doors. Especially Remmy. Last week, I hand a union card to a white sister and she looks at me - from the soles of my hard-toed shoes to the crown of my head. I tell her Remmy asked me to hand-deliver a union card to her and she begins to smile; her smile lights the whole department. What does she do? She signs the union card and hands it to me; she leans in closer to me - so the other white women standing next to her can't hear - and she whispers into my ear, "Remmy aint nothing but a honey-badger." I thank her for signing the card and promised never to stand between her and her honey (*Cast erupts in laughter*).

Cast Member:

Honey-man

Cast:

(*a chorus of "Honey Man" ripples through the church by the entire cast*).

Sam:

Hope you're right. We need our jobs. Me and a lot of other black folk been wearing these union buttons (*touching the union button on his shirt*) since day one. And our white supervisors know we are voting Union; some of them are looking for any reason to fire us. Not all my white supervisors – but some of them; some of them support us but they will never publicize it; the risk belongs solely to us... It's our cross.

Will:

In other plants where employees have pushed the Union, people have been terminated. The Agent at the labor board told us as much.

Sam:

(Walking to the front, turning his back to Will, Remmy and Catherine, addressing the Cast) Remember what happened at Lebo's Canning Company last year: When the Teamsters started organizing the dock workers, managers got wind of it and fired the whole first shift – thirty employees; lead organizers worked the first shift.

Catherine:

But the Teamsters filed a charge with the Labor Board. Those dock workers got their jobs back, along with all back pay and seniority –

Sam:

After a long trial: my pockets ain't deep. I have a mortgage to pay -

Catherine:

(As she approaches the lectern, Will takes a step back so Catherine can address the Cast from the lectern). We all have bills. We're all taking a chance, especially those of us who've been wearing union buttons to work every day. But we have to stand together and fight! With a Union we can do it! From this point forward, even if we lose tomorrow, if any supervisor threatens your job let one of us know. We'll go to the Labor Board and file charges; Board attorneys will fight for us. I know some of you are little afraid of losing your job; I'm concerned about my job too. But we can't sit on the sidelines and do nothing. Our best bet now is to vote union –

Remmy:

Even if it means our jobs, we gotta fight.

Catherine:

We're not only voting for better working conditions and pay for ourselves; we're also voting union for our children. They deserve to work in an environment where they are treated fairly. I don't know about you but *(placing both hands on her stomach)* when my child becomes an adult and asks me "Momma, what did you do to fight racism?" I will be able to lift my head and tell him I fought job discrimination by standing, shoulder-to-shoulder, with my coworkers and voting union. *(The Cast stands, applauds. "Amen!!!!!!!" She returns to her seat and Will returns to his position behind the lectern).*

Will:

Once we vote union tomorrow, we'll have someone at the bargaining table for us, who can push the company to promote women; to promote black people to being supervisors. We want to be promoted just like everyone else. We train new employees, and, three months later, the people we train are supervising us. That's not right. If there are no further questions, I'll see you at the polls tomorrow. After everyone votes, Agents from the Labor Board will count each vote – in our presence. By this time tomorrow, we could have our union in place. Any more questions? Yes, Brother Sam.

Sam:

I started working at Ruby's when I was too young to work at Ruby's; I can't remember the last day I missed a day of work. I know how the company works like I know how to butter my own bread in the morning. Only God knows how many white people I've trained at Ruby's; I can't remember how many I've trained it has been so many. I don't mind it. God gave me a heart to train people. But, this is what pisses me off: Once I've finished training them and correcting their mistakes, I go to work one morning, and the person who I've been training for six weeks is now "my" supervisor (*Sam places both of his hands on his chest)*. Can someone, please, explain to me how you supervise the person who trained you? (*A ripple of "Amens" rise from the Cast*). I know I know the job. Ruby's managers know I know the job. If I didn't know the job, management wouldn't ask me to train. If I know the job then make me the manager because I've earned it. Right? Right? God gave me the skill, the ability, the heart to love the work, then do the right thing and promote me.

Will:

Sam, we've been there. I've trained my own supervisors too; it's not a good feeling to know you've trained someone to make almost twice what you're earning.

Sam:

So, my question is: What can we do about it?

Catherine:

Once we vote union, tomorrow, we can make sure that Ruby's recognizes what you bring to the table and promote you because your talents have made room for you at the table.

Sam:

I ain't begging for no job-

Remmy:

We know – you want what's just and fair. All human beings want what's fair and just. In your case, what the Union can do is make sure Ruby's posts ALL vacant jobs on the bulletin boards in our breakrooms. Brother Sam, did you even know a supervisory position was open, so you could apply for it?

Sam:

Is grits groceries? (*The whole Cast laughs)*. No. Before I finish training them, Ruby's announces that they are promoted to management, right in front of my face. I don't get a 'thank you" for training them.

Remmy:

Like I was saying, we will work with Floyd and design a system Ruby's can use to fill all vacancies at the plant, from maintenance to supervision. (*Sam shakes his head in agreement)* If you've worked at Ruby's most your life like Same and want to promote, your hard work has earned you a place at the table. All vacant jobs should be posted.

Will:

All jobs "must" be posted. We can make it happen. Just vote union. *(While the Cast claps, some chant "Vote Union! Vote Union!!!;" the light goes out on the Stage).*

Act 1 Scene 2

The light comes up on the church, moments later. Will, Catherine and Remmy are tidying up the church, moving chairs, etc.; they are moving freely around the Stage.

Catherine:

The meeting went well, even though some of them looked pretty scared. But I guess scared is good, if you let it focus your eyes on what's important, what needs to be done.

Remmy:

Being scared is part of taking a chance – can't have one without the other. If Ruby's managers learn these folk are supporting the Union they could lose their jobs; that's a chance they're taking, that we're all taking. But, you know you gotta do it; can't turn away from it. It's like when you ask your first girl out on a date: You're hoping she says "yes" –

Will:

And at the same time, you're afraid she may say "no." Good Lord (*He looks up to the ceiling)* – what do I do? She's the prettiest flower in the classroom.

Remmy:

You got to ask her out on a date; you got to ask her to be your girl; if you don't the stars won't ever come out again; and if the stars do come out again at night, they're too small to worry about counting anymore.

Will:

Sometimes they say "yes" and sometimes, "no." But like Remmy said, you gotta try. You gotta ask. You gotta have a girl on your arms.

Remmy:

That's why God created a man's arms, to hold his favorite girl.

Catherine:

I thought he created your arms so you could work and bring some food home to put on the table for your family.

Remmy:

That too, but every man's arms are empty, no matter how much work he's doing with his arms, no matter how much food he's carrying or how many buckets of nails he's lifting, if he has no girl in his arms.

Will:

Honey badger…You think we had some good foot soldiers at the meeting? They seem ready to fight to me.

Remmy:

I got a good feeling about tomorrow …Voting Day. We're looking pretty good, slim and trim. We may just have the number of votes we need in the bag to go Union tomorrow.

Will:

We'll have to keep our eyes open to make sure no one gets fired because they support the union. And not just tomorrow, but for weeks and months to come. My cousin in Chicago works in a meat packing plant; he told me they voted the union in about a year ago. Do you know the managers waited a whole year before they fired the five employees that handed out union cards?

Remmy:

After they voted the union in?

Will:

Yes, 12 months to the day they voted the union in.

Catherine:

I can't believe someone can be that hateful. We will have to watch closely. Floyd can be slippery…

Remmy:

Now you're preaching, sister. You never know how Floyd's mind works. One moment he's sitting on top of the mountain and the next he has a shotgun pointed in your face. He's a new kind of crazy.

Catherine:

We know. That's why we gotta watch him like a hawk, just like Will said.

Will:

Remmy, we'll watch Floyd. I need you to watch our white sisters. You sure they're gonna vote union tomorrow? We're banking on their support. We gotta have it.

Catherine:

We can't have any slip-ups. This may be the only chance we can -

Remmy:

My women won't let me down. I know them and they know me. I'm Remmy. You can trust Remmy. Remmy is the kind of man who notices when a woman loses a little weight and I tell her how beautiful she is, because she is. I notice if she picks up a little weight in the hips and I tell she's even more beautiful because she is. If she sprays on some new perfume, I notice it, and I tell her how sweet she smells.

Catherine:

And what about their husbands – you sniffing around their husbands too?

Remmy:

No, but I promise you: they're working on their husbands, convincing them to vote union, as I speak. Right now -

Catherine:

Preach, Mr. Honeybadger!

Will:

What reasons would their husbands have to support the union? They make more money than we do; they're promoted to supervisor, when we're not. What they stand to gain, unless they're standing on our backs? Ruby's gives them a ham a turkey for Christmas, and we "might" get a dry hen.

Remmy:

My women share pillows with their husbands.

Will:

Is that right -

Catherine:

You don't know where they rest their heads at night?

Remmy:

Pillow talk at night is powerful talk; you plead your case on a soft pillow. You married folk don't know nothing.

Will:

Teach us, Professor -

Remmy:

A preacher can't preach a sermon that can beat soft pillow talk, between a man and a woman. Right before her husband gets what keeps him going all day, she whispers into his ear what she wants: a new pair of shoes from the exclusive women's shop downtown, where the pastor's wife shops. A man is only as good looking as his wife and family. Whispers into his ear she needs a new refrigerator from *Sears & Roebuck* to keep his meat from ruining. (*changing his voice to mimic a woman, he approaches Will to pretend that he is a white woman and Will is her husband; Will is uncomfortable and runs around the Stage to get away from Remmy but pursues him; Catherine holds her stomach and laughs)* Whispers "baby, you know we need a union like we need the sun in the sky.

Sugar, only a real man will vote for the union; and you don't have to tell the other men on the line you voting union. Tomorrow, when you get your ballot and your pencil – you check Union."

Will:

(trying to get away from Remmy, Will runs around stage, laughing, but Remmy pursues him). Gon' man!!! Stop Remmy. Get away from me, Man -

Remmy:

"Baby, after you vote union, bring your little pencil on home to Momma and I'll sharpen your pencil to a fine point; you'll be able to write all night long, all night long…"

Will:

Man, *(laughing)* you crazy.

Remmy:

Soft pillow talk can end wars before they begin, if you let it. Ain't it printed in the Bible? Ain't it one of Moses' commandments? (*The cast laughs and shake their heads)*

Will:

Not any Bible I've read. Honey badger. Maybe in the Bible of Remmy. What you think, Catherine?

Catherine:

(*Catherine bends down to pick up a plant but a contraction strikes*). My God !!!-

Will:

You okay? (*They rush to her side, offering comfort)*

Catherine:

A giant is walking up and down my spine in steel-toed boots. Remmy, can you give a sister a ride?

Remmy:

Will, call Dennis; tell him to meet us at Union Hospital on Poplar; he's about to be a daddy. (*Remmy and Catherine exit, and Will dials the rotary phone).* Dennis? This is Will. I'm fine. Yes…Man, you're about to be a father. Catherine is hanging in there. Remmy is driving her to Union. Yes, my Retha is fine; she's four months pregnant; she got a long way to go. Yes…I'm headed to Union Hospital now. See you later. (*Will returns the telephone to the receiver. Light out, quickly).*

Act 1 Scene 3

The next scene is the first of two scenes in the play that are flashbacks to the 1920s. Light comes up on Ruby and Rueben, who are dancing to an instrumental version of "Bye, Bye Black Bird" by Coltrane and Miles Davis; a version of the song with the actual lyrics would be too literal. Ruby is teaching Rueben to dance. Rueben is dressed rather shabbily, but Ruby wears a beautiful red silk dress with short sleeves. The stage is sparsely furnished: Stage right are two-three small tables pulled together and covered with blueprints, sketches, pencils, an engineering and architectural equipment, etc...

Ruby:

Relax, let your shoulders lean into the music. Now, let the music lift you. Don't fight it. See what happens when you trade those two milk jugs you call feet for to music…my lovely, tone-deaf, Milk Man from New York.

Rueben:

(*He has a very "thick" accent)* Never thought I'd be holding a woman who could afford to wear a different silk dress every day of the week. Until now – every woman I held in my arms wore gingham dresses. Skin never as soft as your skin, smelling like vanilla (*He rubs her arms gently, then inhales her smell, as if trying to pull in everything from her into himself*).

Ruby:

Dancing is not difficult - just relax. Music will never let you fall. It holds you up.

Rueben:

(laughing) Because when you dance you're an angel of light.

Ruby:

Those are not milk jugs (*pointing to his feet*). As of this very moment, you're wearing a rich man's golden, silk slippers. Think light and you'll be dancing in the middle of the air... (*they laugh, he places his head on her shoulder*).

Rueben:

You're a good teacher.

Ruby:

I have a question.

Rueben:

Okay.

Ruby:

Where do you see yourself in the next seven years?

Rueben:

Seven years is a long way off and I count one year at a time.

Ruby:

Seven years can walk like seven days, if you have a plan and you know how to work your plan.

Rueben:

You're the college girl, dancing with a Holstein.

Ruby:

I'm still looking for a professional job. I don't mind waiting tables here at Grace's; this restaurant paid my tuition; bought my books; bought the equipment I needed; bought this new dress. Memphis engineering firms are hiring white males – but not me; not a colored girl. White women who are engineers are hired as secretaries at Engineering firms – not engineers: note takers, not even drafters. Finished at the top of my class, but white guys who finished at the bottom of my class, are getting jobs ahead of me. (*She stops dancing and looks at him*). Let me correct myself…I could get a job at a

Memphis engineering firm, but I would have to sweep floors; clean bathrooms; cook and serve; take out the garbage.

Rueben:

I can go on waiting tables and washing dishes at Grace's. I like it here. I like to hear you sing. I like the people here. Grace's front door is open to everyone who gets off the boat: Jews, blacks, whites, Chinese, Christians, Dutch, German, Italians, folk down on their luck.

Ruby:

What does Pop say?

Reuben:

All folding money is green. I like working here. No waking up at the crack of dawn to milk cows. No shoveling cow-pies. No cows kicking over milk jugs.

Ruby:

My milk man…

Rueben:

When I landed in Memphis a few months ago, I'm so hungry my stomach is reaching for my back. Then, I see a hive of people, buzzing around Grace's. I first thought this is a hotel and the people lining up to pay for a night or two. Then, I walk toward Grace's and I hear your harmonica. I don't have money in my pocket but I don't need money; all I need is your music filling my ears. I may have tin ears, but I know good music when I hear it.

Ruby:

You were hollow inside when you first landed in Memphis. A shell of who you are now...

Rueben:

I'd been closed up for a long time. Not knowing who you are will hurt you and hurt those close to you. Your little, dented harmonica poured light into me. Then, I walk through the door, just when you start to play the piano and singing. Your music walks up behind me, taps me on the shoulder, and asks to see my Soul. Until your music, no one was concerned about sharing any light with me. Until then, no one even cared if I even had a soul.

Ruby:

Trust me?

Rueben:

You and your folks are really the only people I know in America.

Ruby:

Since you trust me – let me dream for both of us.

Rueben:

I need to run something past you.

Ruby:

Okay, but me first. Let me show you something (*She takes his hand and guides him toward the table with the blueprints, but Rueben stops her short to have another conversation).*

Rueben:

I'm been turning this over in my head for the past couple of weeks…I'm thinking about changing my name.

Ruby:

What's wrong with the name you brought to Memphis?

Rueben:

(they laugh) I want to be somebody else in this country. Not a Holstein. But a big man who leaves twenty-dollar dollar tips on the table; who uses a five-dollar bill to light my cigarette.

Ruby:

Why change your name? You look like a Rueben -

Rueben:

You've always wanted your name?

Ruby:

A name is not a cross to bear. Dad named me Ruby cause momma's skin turns a deep ruby color every Fall; in Fall she's in full bloom.

Rueben:

See, you can touch the meaning of your name. I can't

.Ruby:

You ask your momma why she named you Rueben?

Rueben:

She was always seemed to be too busy.

Ruby:

Listen to me, your name don't matter. What matters is how you live the one life God gives you.

Rueben:

You brought light to me; this is my way of marking my new light, accepting it as my light.

Ruby:

(sighing) So, who are you now Mr. Rueben Holstein?

Rueben:

I'm trying this on for size - Franklin R-u-b-i-n-e Holiday. Ruby, I'm wearing your last name the rest of my life.

Ruby:

(*the two kiss; the couple laughs and Ruby takes his hand and walks toward the tables, on which blueprints rest, closer to front of stage-stage right).* I need to tell my parents they have a son. I like Franklin. This (*pointing to the plans)* is why I want to know where you see yourself in the next seven years.

Reuben:

Your pop is teaching me to paint – you need someone to do some painting?

Ruby:

Don't need a painter, Sugar. Our dream is on this table, soaking up the spaghetti sauce from today's special: Ruby's Harmonicas and Pianos, Incorporated. It's finished, except for the harmonica-line I'm still designing. My family is pouring a lot of their life savings into this, but we'll need financing to build a factory. If this goes as I plan, we can employ up to four hundred people when this plant is up and producing. But, we need someone to present this to the Memphis Commercial Bank for a business loan: for start-up money, initial pay roll, contractors, supplies and raw materials. I designed production lines for pianos and I'm designing a new harmonica – first of its kind. I'm using ash wood with mahogany inlay; some harmonicas with ivory inlay. I've finished a business plan, everything we need for financing. I have all the certifications,…Now, this is a two-step process. Initially, we will not produce harmonicas because four piano manufacturers (two in Little Rock, Arkansas; one in Nashville; and one in Jackson, Mississippi) are closing within the next 18 months-

Reuben:

Really?

Ruby:

This is why they're closing: they only produced pianos for high-end markets: Concert halls, wealthy families whose children are headed to Ivy League Colleges. We will not fall into that same trap; I'll design and produce pianos for the pool hall down on Main Street, the juke joint in Georgia, the elementary school in Virginia, and for Carnegie Hall. While we always produce a quality product, we allow the consumer to dictate what particular type of piano they need. I have already spoken with the President at Memphis State and he has already ordered thirty pianos for the music department. But, I have a special job for you, Franklin: Next week, you're gonna meet with the President of the bank and present the plan to him. Dad has granted you access to our savings and checking accounts. In order to get money, you gotta show these white Memphis bankers that you don't need their money.

Reuben:

What!?

Ruby:

Banks don't loan the kind of money we need to poor people. We have to show them we don't need their money. This is how you sell this: (*He walks to the other side of the stage)* you have to let the banker think you're doing his bank a favor by being a part of our enterprise.

Reuben:

What if he asks me a question I can't answer?

Ruby:

Say something like, "It's sharp people like you I want to get in on the ground floor of this new enterprise." Always compliment him and make him feel smart. The more you compliment some white folk, the wider they will open their wallets and purses.

Reuben:

I'm white and my pockets are empty –

Ruby:

Baby, you're not a white man; You're fresh off the boat. (*She walks in his direction)* The first time you walked into Grace's you asked Dad if he had any cows needed milking. Honey, when I kiss you I still taste sea salt (*she walks up behind him, hugs him; he drops his head and then they laugh. Then he turns around and they hold each other)*.

Reuben:

My people have been getting paid by the pail for hundreds of years. This is high finance. This banker will smell the sea salt on my skin.

Ruby:

Not after we wash you down with lye soap. My mom got a new batch.

Reuben:

I've only negotiated for a larger pail to hold more milk.

Ruby:

We're not buying by the pail and selling by the pail. You can't be timid---not now. I need you full of piss and vinegar when you walk into his office.

Reuben:

(*noticeably nervous and unsure of himself*) I don't know, Ruby. What if you come with me?

Ruby:

This is the deep south: a black woman's place is pushing a broom, not designing a piano line. We're not supposed to know anything about a business plan. If I walk into the bank president's office with you, we will not get the loan. What are you full of?

Reuben:

Piss and vinegar. But I'm a milk man –

Ruby:

Not anymore; not after today. You got a new name. From now on, you light your pipe with ten-dollar bills. When you walk into his office, the Banker's secretary needs to say, 'Who is this man, walking in here, as if he has a million dollars in his discretionary account?' Understand?

Reuben:

Yes…(*light fades*).

Act 2 Scene 1

(Light comes up in Floyd's office, sparsely furnished: Floyd's desk and two chairs face his desk; a long conference table, center stage; a credenza with family photos, plaques, etc. Will and Remmy are seated at one end of the table). A month has passed since the election.

Will:

What's happening in the Main Conference room – barely elbow room? Everybody's smiling, reporters interviewing Floyd, photographers snapping pictures. Floyd running for Governor of Tennessee?

Remmy:

A gubernatorial seat is beneath Floyd. Earlier, I saw a cake shaped like a baby grand piano, near the receptionist's desk. Maybe it's somebody's birthday. Let's keep our heads in the game.

Will:

It's been a month and Floyd still pissed we voted the union into Ruby's.

Remmy:

Being angry is a weakness when you negotiating. Let's hope he keeps it up.

Will:

I gotta give to you, Honey Badger. You delivered the votes, man.

Remmy:

I know women.

Will:

Who filling in for Catherine? We need a real good Note-taker. I know chickens who hold a pencil and scratch-out a better sentence than you, my friend.

Remmy:

My woman don't love me cause of my handwriting. She likes how I handle the pencil I was born with; *that* pencil makes her smile.

Will:

(Will laughs, rises, then walks to a water pitcher in the middle of the table, pours a cup of water): Want a glass? (*Remmy nods his head no)* What about Catherine's temporary replacement?

Remmy:

His name is Bryan DuBose. (*Looking at his watch)* he'll be here.

Will:

DuBose?

Remmy:

Works third shift – family man – don't drink liquor – don't chase women. Top production man at Ruby's last year. No disciplines. Comes to work, on time, and the last one to clock-out.

Will:

DuBose sign a union card?

Remmy:

I think Catherine got him to sign one of her cards. He's huge - could probably carry a baby grand on his back to Alabama and back.

Will:

From Alabama?

Remmy:

He's from Selma, Alabama; they say he tried to cross Edmund Pettus Bridge...all three times.

Will:

He marched on Bloody Sunday. Police cracked a lot of skulls: men, women, black, whites, Catholics, Baptists, Unitarians, Episcopalians, Methodists. Police cracked a lot of heads that day, regardless of your affiliations.

Remmy:

Bloodiest day since Christ bled-out on the cross.

Will:

You ain't no Christian – what do you know about a cross?

Remmy:

I may not be a Christian, but I know about carrying a cross across your shoulders: a black man born in this country birthed with a cross, whether he wants the cross or not. DuBose carried his cross from Selma to the steps of the capital in Montgomery.

Will:

Sounds like a committed man and he's what we need, though Catherine ain't no joke herself. If this country wasn't so screwed up, Catherine would be someone's attorney right now. Our black congressmen, doctors, scientists, college professors, and judges sweeping & mopping floors; picking up and emptying garbage cans; cleaning buildings and taking care of other folks' children.

Remmy:

Amen (*mockingly)*. Preach, Pastor! (*lifting both of his hands)* Praise the Lord (*the two laugh*)!

Will:

You're a *foot-soldier for the devil*. What else do I need to know about this Mr. DuBose.

Remmy:

Everybody calls him "Radio."

Will:

We need a tough-nosed negotiator at this (*rubbing and then patting the table)* bargaining table. Why they call him Radio?

Remmy:

Say he don't play the Radio, a serious brother. (*There is a* ***thunderous*** *knock on the door and Radio enters; he's confident, poised; he has a briefcase. The three men shake hands*).

Will:

Radio, you trying to buy a door?

Remmy:

You knocking on that door like it's yours.

Radio:

My sweat paid for that door and every door at Ruby's, so, I guess it's my property. If I had a screwdriver, I'd unhinge it and take it home…I need a new door to my outhouse *(Remmy and Will laugh).*

Will:

Our newest member of the Union's negotiating team. Now, I remember you from church..., sitting on the front row.

Remmy:

Radio, how's your family?

Radio:

(He takes a seat, begins to slowly unpack his briefcase, removing pads, ink pins, pencils, etc.) Good – good – Lisa and I have seven boys. Good hearts *(smiling)* but hard-headed like daddy.

Remmy:

Will, you are looking at a man who knows how to write with the pencil God gave him *(they laugh).*

Radio:

Ain't about a pencil, but sunshine.

Will:

What shine?

Radio:

My boys bring light into my life. Each one of them: Every day – each in their own way. My life was empty and black - until I met my Lisa. Family's the reason I get up in the morning, and work like a Hebrew slave - building pianos I can't afford. I wake my sons, early in the morning: I kiss each one on the forehead. My daddy always woke me with a kiss on the forehead when I was a little boy; I still feel each kiss; I believed the sun wouldn't rise if dad did not kiss me on the forehead. So, I kiss my seven sons early in the morning to raise the sun in the sky.

Remmy:

Man…-

Radio:

Seconds later they rush through the house, flushing every room with sunlight... Sometimes I don't even need to switch the light on. Until I was a father, I hadn't felt such light outside church. I was on the Mourner's bench in Selma for three straight years. And one day I accepted Christ; he brought so much light into my life I almost drowned in sunshine.

Will:

My wife Retha and I expecting our first child. I'm expecting that same light.

Radio:

You give light – you get light. The light focuses my eyes on what counts in life…

Will:

Radio, I was wondering - how you got your union card – from Catherine? Some folk were afraid to sign a card, black and white.

Radio:

I walk into this office and Floyd is sitting behind his desk. I ask for union card and extend my hand.

Will:

Really!!!? Just like that -

Remmy:

Radio, stop blowing smoke up Will's skirt (*all laugh*).

Will:

You bold, man. What Floyd do?

Radio:

He reaches in his top right drawer (*pointing in the direction of Floyd's desk*) and pulls out a union card; he has a stack of them. I ask for a pen. I read the front and back of the card: Write my information on the card - I sign it. Give Floyd back his pen, slip the card in my shirt pocket, and leave, closing "my door" behind me (*they laugh*). When I see Catherine later on, I hand it to her.

Remmy:

R-a-d-i-o!!!!

Will:

Most people were afraid for Ruby's to know they support the union, but you walk into the office of the man who owns the plant (*Floyd enters*).

Floyd:

Excuse my lateness; if this wasn't my office I would have knocked before entering.

Radio:

Especially for our first negotiation session.

Floyd:

(*He walks to his desk; there are three chairs in front of his desk, but Radio, Remmy and Will continue to sit at the table, center stage*): Mr. DuBose, didn't know you were on the union's bargaining committee?

Radio:

I'm just sitting in until Catherine comes back.

Floyd:

I just heard she lost the baby. She'll be coming back soon, having exhausted her sick leave.

Will:

What if she needs more time – it being her first child?

Floyd:

She can go on un-paid leave if she needs more time: We make harmonicas and pianos at Ruby's – not babies. Will, I'm not running a hospital. (*He retrieves a thirty-page document from the same drawer he had retrieved a union card for Radio*). OK – here's our labor contract. (*Floyd walks to the table, and slides the contract across the table to the three men*). Let's just sign this and get back to work. *(Remmy, Radio and, Will look at one another in disbelief and then they all look at Floyd, who is still standing)*

Remmy:

Floyd, what in God's name - ?!

Floyd:

A labor contract. Some people call it a collective bargaining agreement, a CBA. I call it an unnecessary intrusion into Ruby's personnel affairs. But, I'm not the Labor Board.

Will:

Floyd, you understand we are here to negotiate a labor contract: proposals, counter proposals, bargaining across the table –

Floyd:

To save everyone time and money –

Will:

This ain't how this works, Floyd. We negotiating everything: From the number of sick leave days –

Remmy:

To the size of our annual raises.

Radio:

From the number and length of our breaks, to the hours in our work-week.

Will:

Floyd, you've wasted some good paper - (*balancing the contract in his hands).*

Floyd:

(*Taking a seat at the opposite end of the bargaining table*): I've already signed it. Just sign on the last page –

Will:

This contract good for one thing, Floyd – wrapping fish.

Radio:

Wrap fish or wipe your butt with it. Either way - we're not signing it. Floyd, will Ruby's attorney negotiate with us or will it be just you?

Floyd:

I told the Board of Directors this labor contract is "Floyd's baby" and I have the final say. In the proverbial words of Charlton Heston in the movie *"Moses,"* 'So, let it be written, so let it be done.'

Will:

In the proverbial words of James Brown, "I feel good. I knew I would. So good/So good…we got you..." (*Radio and Remmy begin to laugh, but Floyd has a puzzled look).*

Floyd:

It seems my initial proposal has been rejected?

Radio:

Rejected. So let it be written, so let it be done.

Floyd:

Who's taking minutes?

Radio:

(Removing pencil and paid from his briefcase and taking notes). Me.

Floyd:

Before we roll up our sleeves and begin hard-nosed negotiations, I have a brief Opening Statement. *(Floyd stands, walks around the stage like he's a professor lecturing a freshman class; the more he talks, the more he transforms into a white southern, fire-and-brimstone preacher).* Ruby's is a family business, lovingly passed down from my grandfather to my father and from my father to me - in Spirit and in Truth. I represent the third generation. We bring music into existence, into the lives of Americans. *(He walks to his desk and retrieves a picture of his grandfather),* I draw your attention to Ruby's Exhibit Number One: our founder, my grandfather, Franklin Rubine Holiday. Because of his instrument, pianos grace the halls of colleges, universities, town halls, schools; in the private homes of aristocrats, as well as Memphis juke joints. *(Floyd is becoming intoxicated from his own words)* I will not recline in my grave, until one of our pianos are perched in the White House. I announce to you today *(a preacher strolling around his pulpit)* we're on the verge of exporting our musical gems internationally: Before the Chinese eat a spoonful of rice, they will stroke the keys of a baby-grand. In South America, before those people sink their teeth into a taco, they will stroke a baby-grand. It's too hot for pianos in Africa so we will forego exporting to Africa at this time. *(The bargaining team members sit back in their chairs and let Floyd preach his sermon).* Ruby's Exhibit Number Two: Ruby's is pregnant with expectation. Let's be sure to include "We are Pregnant With Expectation" in the bargaining notes, Mr. Radio.

Radio:

Duly noted, Floyd.

Floyd:

(*Turning his back to the men; he replaces the photograph of his grandfather, then picks up a photograph of his father and begins to speak to the photograph).* Father, we are pregnant - Tumbling Big, with honor, truth, and family history. And our "water" is about to break (*bargaining committee members shake their heads in disbelief).* We are dedicated to producing supreme harmonicas and pianos. *(now picking up photograph of grandfather again. Now, he has a picture in each hand).*We're here because my grandfather had a musical dream: Franklin Rubine Holiday!!, a self-made man. God bless him.

Will:

Floyd, Floyd...

Floyd:

Excuse me, Will, but this is my Opening Statement. Mr. Radio, are you getting every word?

Radio:

Carry on, Floyd.

Floyd:

My grandfather was a man of sheer music. *(Returning the picture of his father to the desk)* A musical genius. Engineer. Architect. Designer of Harmonicas and Pianos. An artist who spoke in wood. A trained Engineer and architect who drafted the plans for the design of our plant. No greater man has ever lived, including Charlton Heston. This morning, as a testament to Mr. Holiday's genius and industrial foresight, I dedicated the hallway up front *(looking and kissing the photograph of his grandfather)* to you grandfather. From today throughout eternity, the hallway up front will be called the "Gold Mile." Charlton Heston had his Red Sea and my grandfather now has his Gold Mile. I invite each of you and members of your families to stroll his Gold Mile.

This is what you will see: behind locked, glass-enclosed panels and boxes, you will see original blue- prints Mr. Holiday designed with his own hands; when he died he still had blue smudges on his fingers from studying and handling his blue prints from morning until evening; his blue prints were holy scripture to him. You will see his picture and the picture of the woman who stood next to him, the daughter of the Memphis banker who financed Ruby's. God bless her. This young couple were musical dreamers; at night their heads shared the same pillow; their pillow talk carved out a musical empire, … without comparison. What was their dream? I'm glad you asked, Mr. Radio: to produce harmonicas and pianos the angels in heaven would love to purchase to serenade God.

Remmy:

Floyd, we have to –

Floyd:

Mr. Holiday was a man of heavenly principles: A lie never rested on his lips; he was the salesman's salesman. Radio, did you get my last quote? Holy commercial scripture could have flowed from his lips, on a daily basis, but he never had a note-taker; Mr. Radio, if only you were alive when he walked the earth...you could have greatly served him.

Radio:

(taking notes) I got it, Floyd, "holy commercial scripture." I've started looking into your family's history and it's interesting.

Floyd:

Let me know what you find. I plan to write a biography of my family. Radio, check us out, we are a family of virtue and craft. Take my grandmother, a woman before her time (*Floyd replaces the picture of his grandfather on his desk and selects a photo of his grandmother and allows them to see,* ***but not touch*** *the picture; Floyd places the picture on his desk)*. By the time she'd met my grandfather, her heels were indeed round. I was recently at a business meeting and I overheard a man of industry compliment her. Speaking of my grandmother, he said, "she gave it out of both pants legs." What did he mean? She gave her life to help the needy. God rest her soul in heaven! I believe Mr. Remmy wants to know about the future of the company?

Remmy:

Floyd, please stop reading my mind…

Floyd:

We employ over three-hundred people here and we're ramping up to hire more (*Floyd is truly preaching now)*. We have a plant in Birmingham, Alabama, employing three-hundred-and-fifty; a plant in New Orleans employing another three hundred; plants in North and South Carolina each employing two hundred. We break ground for a new manufacturing plant in Nashville within the next twelve months. These new openings are in keeping with Ruby's slogan: "Our harmonicas and pianos walk up behind you, tap you on your shoulder, and ask to see your soul." This slogan chiseled on grandfather's tombstone. Eventually, his tombstone will serve as the crown jewel of the Gold Mile – that's my plan… grandfather wasn't the only visionary in this family.

Will:

(*standing*)Floyd, let's discuss ground rules for negotiations this morning.

Floyd:

Duly-noted. What follows is Ruby's Exhibit Number Three: my Closing Statement (*Will reclaims his seat, shaking his head in disbelief*). Mr. Radio, I hope you still have a fine point on your pencil so you can keep up with me.

Radio:

My pencil is pointed…

Floyd:

(Pointing in the direction of the hallway) Men, in closing, I welcome you to walk the Gold Mile. I was a little late this morning, because I was dedicating the Gold Mile. The Mayor was here. Along with his lovely wife, their beautiful children, and their two dogs, Lou Lou and Sandman. At the dedication, I announced we had been awarded federal contracts to manufacture pianos for the Navy, Army, and the Marines. The only thing we have to do is keep our noses clean. Who knows – maybe we can soon manufacture harmonicas and pianos for the Air Force too.

Radio:

Floyd, in the future, it would be nice to invite the employees to grand openings like the Gold Mile – since we make the pianos.

Floyd:

We will be opening the Gold Mile for tours later this fall. Ruby's is the centerpiece for the City's **Builders Of The Memphis Bluff Initiative**: All residents who've made key contributions to establishing Memphis as an industrial powerhouse will be honored with a plaque (*Floyd reclaims his seat at the bargaining table).* My family's name claims the first spot on the plaque hanging in City Hall.

Will:

I'm sure your family is proud. Let's get down to business. I spoke with a production employee; she told me today she when approached the lady's room, near your Gold Mile, a security guard blocked her entrance into the lady's room -

Remmy:

She asks the guard why she couldn't enter the lady's room, he said there was a "new" rule at Ruby's: She has to use the bathroom nearest her production line. Floyd - what new rule?

Radio:

You can't make any new company rules affecting the employees, without first bargaining with us; we represent them now.

Floyd:

She's referencing the *Rule of Efficiency & Production* that I drafted last night. The rule is to protect her by decreasing the number of steps she navigates in steel-toed shoes, adding years to life and limb. Ruby's official position is we don't bargain with the union about such personal rules.

Radio:

A rule is a rule.

Remmy:

Okay - explain why you believe this new rule is an exception?

Floyd:

Let's say, Mr. Radio *(pointing to Radio)*, who works in production needs to relieve himself. Well, he wastes too much production time walking to the Gold Mile in his heavy, steel-toed shoes. He can use the bathroom in the production department, adding years to his life and limbs.

Will:

Until this morning – we could use any bathroom we wanted to use in this plant. Correct?

Floyd:

Seems like an accurate statement.

Remmy:

Why the change?

Floyd:

Not to speak over your heads - but it's a matter of productivity. Once the public tours start, the public will visit the Golden Mile. They may need a little privacy when they go to the bathroom. Like I said, -

Radio:

We heard you the first time – a Rule of Efficiency & Production. But Floyd you can't make any changes at Ruby's impacting us without bargaining with us.

Remmy:

Floyd, piss is piss. I don't care if it comes out of a visitor or someone working in the plant.

Radio:

When you flush, it all goes to the same place.

Floyd:

But this rule makes sense.

Remmy:

Let's try this another way. Floyd, as a little kid, you had trouble learning how to read and write; me and the fellows on the production line started writing big block letters on wood scraps. Remember?

Floyd:

I recollect, but I can't be for sure.

Remmy:

We would write a letter on a throw-away piece of wood, then you would copy what we wrote on the same piece of wood.

Floyd:

I understand – go on.

Remmy:

By the time you learned how to spell your first name, we had written on practically every piece of scrap wood in the plant. Your momma was as pleased as punch, but your daddy was pissed cause he had better uses for the scrap wood. Then, one day he announces, "No more writing on scrap wood for Floyd; let him learn like other kids, writing on black slate in a classroom." But me and a few men in production pulled your old man aside; explained to your dad we couldn't suddenly stop writing on wood – this was us negotiating for you Floyd – you see? we had to slowly wean you off wood and onto slate. A sudden change would have shocked your system…you would have never learned to spell Holiday. You see? We negotiated for you -

Floyd:

Okay.

Remmy:

Floyd, this is the same thing: The Piano Makers Union represent all employees at Ruby's, just like we represented you. No new rules without first bargaining with us. It does not matter if you believe the rule makes the company more productive –

Radio:

or less productive –

Will:

True.

Remmy:

Your dad should have discussed the new rule with us before he made any changes; likewise, you have to meet, discuss, and bargain any new rule with us.

Will:

Anything impacting hours, wages, and conditions of employment, Floyd. Let's do this: We will have another meeting next week. We'll both bring proposals, and we will be ready to make some decisions. Floyd, the next time you issue a new rule, we will have no choice but to file a charge with the Labor Board. Now, are you gonna rescind that new bathroom rule?

Floyd:

Ruby's can't have any charges filed with the Labor Board; such charges would impact our new contracts with the Armed forces. Next week, I'm framing those contracts and hanging them on the Gold Mile; these contracts are my contribution to the history of Ruby's.

Radio:

Listen to the man, Floyd, don't run off writing new rules on paper, wood scraps, black slate or on anything else, unless you want us to file charges with the federal Labor Board.

Floyd:

We'll see – But I can't commit on paper - right now. I'm considering my options (*light fades, with Radio shaking his head in disbelief) Light goes down.*

Act 2 Scene 2

(A week later. The light comes up on Floyd's office; he is walking around the office, dusting family trinkets, pictures, plaques, etc., with a bright white cloth).

Floyd:

(There is a knock at the door). Come in...*(enters Radio with a brown package big enough to hold a student text book).* How can I help you, Mr. Radio?

Radio:

Good morning, Floyd. (*Radio takes a seat in a chair near Floyd's desk)*

Floyd:

(He continues polishing) I'm impressed with you… the only Ruby employee who walked into my office and asked me for a union card. You're worth watching! Good Lord, you're worth watching. How can I help?

Radio:

You can help us with better treatment at Ruby's: If white employees and black employees have the same seniority, working the same job, we should get the same pay – it's only fair.

Floyd:

(He continues dusting family pictures, etc., moving to his desk). Why should your needs be my needs? My needs are what wake me up in the morning. A man's needs belong to him – alone. How would you like it, if I handed you my light bill, and asked you to pay my light bill? I need light to find my gold slippers; my children need light so they can read. But it's my house needing light – not yours. Your house may be lit up like a Christmas tree or black dark. But, that's your need, not my need. A blind man can see what I'm talking about. See what I mean? Be careful not to mix up your needs with my needs -

Radio:

Sounds like a threat…?

Floyd:

Just joking…relax. It's beneath my station to threaten a member of the union's organizing committee. *(He hands Radio a plaque).* My grandfather won this national award from the Piano Manufacturing Society in New York. He won it so many times they named it after him. Am I from good stock, Mr. Radio?

Radio:

It seems Memphis and the whole country impressed with your family's accomplishments. (*He returns the plaque to Floyd, who feverishly wipes the award with the cloth, as if to wipe off Radio's fingerprints).* Why hide this family jewel in your office, what about the Gold Mile?

Floyd:

Good idea. This goes on the Gold Mile this afternoon. Now, *(taking his seat behind his desk but continuing to polish the plaque)*, again, how can I help you?

Radio:

(*Up to now, Floyd has failed to notice the package Radio has in his lap. For the rest of the scene, Floyd is captivated with the package and Radio shifts the package from his lap to the floor, from the floor to the chair to his right, to the chair to his left, back to his lap; by the end of the Scene, Floyd is hypnotized by the package; whenever Radio moves the package, Floyd's eyes follow the package.)* Last week, with the opening of the Gold Mile and the fact it will soon be visited by the general public, I got to thinking...

Floyd:

(He stops rubbing the plaque and looks at Radio). Yes? *(Floyd replaces the plague on his desk and picks up another family trinket from his desk and begins to polish it; throughout the balance of the Scene, Floyd polishes one trinket or another.)*

Radio:

I enjoyed my visit to your Gold Mile: enjoyed the photographs, letters, original blueprints and plans for the plant, but I have a few questions.

Floyd:

Okay – *(Floyd becomes overjoyed)* you're researching my family's history? I'm a man of history because history is composed of cold, hard facts. You can flirt with history, but history won't change; you can try to lie on history, but history won't change. You can curse history, but it won't stop being history. History always gets a rise out of me. In another life, I would be a history professor at Harvard, Yale. Mr. Radio, I have a confession: I'm a fool for the printed page. Okay, what are your questions? (*Immediately the atmosphere between the two men transforms into a murder trial and Floyd, who is testifying, is the murderer, and Radio is the prosecutor, careful, nuanced)*.

Radio:

Your grandfather, Franklin Rubine Holiday, lands on Ellis Island, with only a harmonica in his pocket, correct?

Floyd:

One harmonica – but not one red cent.

Radio:

Lands on Ellis Island "after" 1900, correct?

Floyd:

Exactly – not earlier. You're an excellent fact checker. Mr. Radio, are you a fool of history too (*smiling*)?

Radio:

Your grandfather landed on Ellis Island, but his real name was Rueben Holstein - not Franklin Rubine Holiday.

Floyd:

What? (*Looking perplexed)*

Radio:

Floyd, you're a Holstein – not a Holiday.

Floyd:

*(shocked)*Holstein! Are you sure?

Radio:

Listen, (*Radio moves his package to a chair and Floyd's eyes begin to follow the package)* between 1892 and 1954, when an immigrant arrives on Ellis Island they met with inspectors from the immigration service. During immigrant processing, he completes Immigration Form 711, which asks each immigrant the following questions: What is his name, occupation, how much money he had in his pockets. Because of a fire, a new Ellis Station is built around 1900, and all records "before" 1900 are destroyed; this fact is important. We know your grandfather arrives after 1900 from the Dutch province of North Holland, because I found his record.

Floyd:

How are you so sure you read grandfather's Form seven-eleven?

Radio:

According to his immigration record hanging on your Gold Mile, he was seventeen when he arrives on a Dutch ship called *Lazarus. Lazarus* transports premium lye soap to New York hospitals. According to ship records, all the males who arrive during this particular three-week period were married and over 35 years of age. Are you following me, Floyd?

Floyd:

"Show me," said the blind man.

Radio:

During this three-week period, a local New York Newspaper reports a seventeen-year-old male, Dutch immigrant stows away in the hold of *Lazarus*. It seems during the voyage, he'd slept between crates of lye soap, and his name is Rueben Holstein – not Franklin Rueben Holiday. The title of the newspaper article? "Holstein Chooses To Lie with Lye Soap To Make His American Dream Come True."

Floyd:

Was he a young entrepreneur?

Radio:

Holstein's Form 711 lists his occupation is "Milker" and his only possession is a Milking Jug.

Floyd:

Why would he need to mention an occupation?

Radio:

If an immigrant did not have an occupation, he would have been deported back to his country. Federal officials consider the person unemployable, a vagrant. So, immigrants have to convince federal officials that they have a skill. Your grandfather was a professional milk man.

Floyd:

How can you be so sure?

Radio:

No other Holstein lands on Ellis Island for the next five years, Floyd.

Floyd:

I'm not impressed with your evidence.

Radio:

History is facts –

Floyd:

Not in this case – maybe you've misread something

Radio:

True, so I begin researching the family name "Holiday" in Memphis archives (*Radio returns the package to his lap and Floyd's eyes follow the package)* and my search leads me to the special **Black Family Section** at the Memphis Public Library. (*Radio stands with the package and begins walking the office, articulating a closing statement in a death penalty case before a jury).*This archive includes a Trail Blazers Section: pictures of Black Americans, who were born in Memphis, and made great contributions to the areas of art, business, and medicine.

Floyd:

You have a discerning nose, Mr. Radio. Got bloodhound in your bloodline?

Radio:

One photograph features a young black woman, who is also the first black person to graduate from Memphis State University; she earns dual degrees in both engineering and architecture. To this day, she is the only woman to ever finish the college with dual degrees in engineering and architecture; she completed both degrees in just in four years. Floyd, her name is Ruby Holiday, and Ms. Holiday wrote an unpublished autobiography about her life.

Floyd:

Okay.

Radio:

Ms. Holiday was an only child and her parents owned a restaurant called *Grace's Place* at 1529 Main, which is located a few blocks from the Memphis shipyard: Many a lonely traveler disembark every day. Floyd, think about it? Her name is Ruby and the first word in the name of this company is Ruby –

Floyd:

And my grandfather's name is Rubine. You don't have to be an anthropologist to scratch Ruby's out of Rubine – the two names sound basically the same. In this country, men name their companies after women, everyday. Every hurricane is named after a woman – didn't you know? Hurricane Ruby.

Radio:

Maybe he names (*still pacing and placing the package on the bargaining table)* the company after Ruby. Think about it –

Floyd:

Don't have to think about it. He birthed this company and he could've named it whatever he wanted to name it: Lazarus Harmonicas & Pianos, Boaz Harmonicas & Pianos. A mere coincidence; nothing more. What good stuff did you find?

Radio:

Floyd, is it another coincidence your last name, Holiday, is the same name as Ruby's? If it's a mere coincidence then I'm a bucket of Kentucky Fried Chicken. According to form seven-eleven, your last name should be Holstein – not Holiday (*he picks up the package from the table and Floyd's eyes are trained on the package).*

Floyd:

Wouldn't be the first time federal agents misspelled a name of an immigration form. Let's relax, Radio. Let's think through this: If I hear you correctly, this is based on an "unpublished" autobiography? One copy?

Radio:

Correct.

Floyd:

If Ms. Holiday's book has not been published – it's only good for wrapping fish.

Radio:

It's written in her own words -

Floyd:

Follow me, Radio. We're reasonable men. Book publishers are in the business of publishing books, making a profit. And the tale you're spinning would have made some publisher rich - if it was true.

Radio:

Floyd, (*Radio reclaims his seat in front of Floyd's desk*) the book was not published because someone (and I don't know who) evidently convinced a local Memphis judge to issue a Temporary Restraining Order (TRO). This TRO blocked Memphis-based Guiding Light Books from publishing Ms. Holiday's autobiography. A copy of the Judge's Order is included with Ms. Holiday's records in the Archives at the public library; the actual order is difficult to read because it is frayed and torn -

Floyd:

(stuttering, floundering; Floyd is onboard the Titanic and it's beginning to sink) Follow me, Radio, Good Lord. (*Floyd rises from his desk and paces the office)* We have no evidence my grandfather ever met this woman, Ruby Holiday. Maybe a Memphis judge grants the TRO because Ms. Holiday is simply trying to take credit for my grandfather's hard-work? Maybe she is nothing but a black leech!!!, (*Radio slowly shakes his head "no")* trying to steal my grandfather's plans, his life's work? Trying to ruin the sterling reputation of a good white man? Radio, did it cross your mind - Ruby is a fraud?

Radio:

I thought about it. You got access to your grandfather's records?

Floyd:

True.

Radio:

(Now standing) All important documents hanging on the Gold Mile.

Floyd:

You're right, everything.

Radio:

Alongside Ms. Holiday's picture at the library is her college degree, as well as her professional certifications. However, there's no evidence your grandfather ever attended Memphis State, or any other college. How can a man, who had milked cows, design not only a plant, but also design original plans for pianos and harmonicas? Not to mention the necessary funding? Floyd, he stowed away between crates of lye soap. Floyd, this is the question you need to ask yourself: Why are his degrees not displayed on the Gold Mile? Where are his certifications – the blueprints and plan for Ruby's had to be approved -

Floyd:

Maybe my grandmother buried his degrees with him? Radio, would you like me to dig up his casket to see if he buried his degrees and certifications with him? I can do it! I can resurrect him!!

Radio:

I checked the yearbooks at Memphis State. There's not one engineering or architectural graduate with the name Holstein or a Franklin R. Holiday. Also, the name of this company is Ruby's Harmonicas and Pianos, but I can't find one record establishing we've ever manufactured harmonicas. Pianos, yes, -but not one harmonica, why? You have always told us your grandfather landed on Ellis Island with only a harmonica in his pocket. I would think, since he loved harmonicas, he would have devoted a sizeable portion of the company to making harmonicas.

Floyd:

(Floyd's arguments are losing traction and he knows it) Pianos are our niche market. We have never produced saxophones but we could, also flutes, horns, trumpets or tambourines in the future. We've always intended to manufacture harmonicas: Check the Gold Mile – facts don't lie. My grandfather designed and drafted blueprints with harmonica production in mind; he was an industrial

prophet. As a matter of fact, I will issue a press release tomorrow, announcing we're expanding our production line to include harmonicas.... *(Floyd takes his seat behind his desk again; his disposition changes).* Radio, I see what's happening here. You've been *a busy beaver,* researching my family, misinterpreting facts you stole from the Gold Mile, pin-pointing dates of arrival, occupations, spinning lies... *(Floyd laughs, leans back in his chair)* So, how much is it gonna cost me to bury what you've found? *(Floyd reaches in a drawer and withdraws a checkbook)* I knew I would have no choice but to respect you: the man from Selma, Alabama, who had marched across the Edmund Pettus Bridge – all three times. Walks into my office, just like you're crossing another a Bridge; asks me for a Union Card. All the other black people afraid to let me know they support the union, but not you. Not Mr. Bloody Sunday *(Floyd picks up a pen and begins filling out a check)* How much?

Radio:

Didn't spend my time shaking your family tree to blackmail you. Ain't about money, Floyd; it's about righting a wrong your grandfather committed and your family still profits from: He stole this black woman's ideas, passed them off as his own, and he became a millionaire; there's no record he gave Ms. Holiday one red cent of the profits. No one goes from milking cows to designing a manufacturing plant with no proper training. No one goes from carrying a milk jug to designing a piano.

Floyd:

(violently slamming his hand on his desk) What kind of fool do you take me to be!? I didn't land on Ellis Island this morning. I'm a businessman – not a Milk Man. *(picking up his telephone receiver)* I can telephone any bank president in a four-state area and get a million-dollar line of credit. Just with my word...God can't do that!!! I can telephone the Memphis Police Chief, who attends my church, and explain a nosey employee is trying to blackmail me. *(Returning the telephone to the receiver)*I could give him your address, and before you make it home, I can destroy your whole life…with one call. Jesus can't do that!!!!!

Radio:

I'm not for sale! While you're riffling-off press releases, write a release giving credit for the success of this company to Ruby Holiday. Since you wanna write a check, consider writing a few checks to her family.

Floyd:

What's in the package you been cuddling in your lap, like it's a baby?

Radio:

This grown-folk business.

Floyd:

Listen closely, this is a direct order: pass it to me.

Radio:

(Standing up, holding the package and facing Floyd) No.

Floyd:

I don't like repeating myself: This is a direct order from the owner of Ruby's: hand the package to me – right now.

Radio:

(*walking towards the door to leave*): Floyd, the only person who sees "my package" is my wife.

Floyd:

If you leave, I'm terminating you for failing to follow a direct order. (*Radio departs the office; light fades. Intermission)*

Act 2 Scene 3

(The light comes up in a Memphis Bank President's office; the same actor who plays Floyd also plays the Memphis Banker. The banker's desk is Center Stage and there is one leather arm chair in front of his desk. Franklin, seated in the arm chair, is dressed in a dark colored suit of the period, sporting a red tie, a fresh haircut. His shoulders are drawn back; he looks like a millionaire. The Bank President, who is tall and overweight, is standing Stage Left with blue prints in his hand, obviously impressed with the plans.)

Banker:

(holding up the blueprints to the light). Mr. Holiday, is it?

Reuben:

Franklin Rubine Holiday.

Banker:

A name you wear well *(stealing a quick look at Holiday)*. Such a name prints well on a paycheck, a business card. *(Walking around with the plans)* I'm impressed and I'm not easily impressed. I've had many men walk through my door, asking for loans to finance crazy, doomed enterprises; everything from rose-colored sunglasses for roosters to life insurance policies for dogs.

Reuben:

Some men don't value your time and talent, kind sir.

Banker:

I love someone who measures his words before he opens his mouth; too many people walk around Memphis, writing checks with their mouths and I know they don't have one red cent in the bank. Mr. Holiday, you're the kind of man to make Memphis one of the great cities in the South. These plans are almost too perfect: Where did you get your training? They're almost like art.

Reuben:

I'm from New York.

Banker:

I'm a southerner, but I have to admit, colleges up north turn out better students than we southerners do.

Reuben:

Given your insight – I'd assumed you were northern-trained, a man of your intellect.

Banker:

I'm a southern boy to the bone. Can count on one hand how many times I've left the South. I love Memphis - God bless it. Mr. Holiday, you are a man of grand ideas: Which will you produce first, harmonicas or pianos?

Reuben:

Since four piano plants in the region will be closing their doors within a year from now, I'll produce pianos first. Once we get up and going, then harmonicas in ash wood; some with mahogany inlay; some with fourteen karat inlay.

Banker:

Your ear is to the ground: I only heard about those closings myself. Kind sir, I'm about to ask you a question. It's a world-changing question. If you died tonight, and you answer this question wrong, it could make the difference between spending all eternity tossing and turning on a bed of hot coals, or spending millions of years singing and praising the Lord Jesus: You ready for the question?

Reuben:

Sir?

Banker:

Are you a Christian? If I'm sweeping too close to your front door with the question, just tell me, and I will sweep somewhere else.

Reuben:

In this country, I understand a lot of stock in placed in this fellow Jesus. I understand.....

Banker:

Religion ain't just a head thing *(pointing to his head)*, but it's about (*moving his hand to his heart*),…the heart. You can't think your way into heaven. If that was the case, there wouldn't be one black person, male or female, in heaven. It's about your heart, opening your heart, just like you open up your jacket, and asking our sweet Jesus (blue eyes and blond hair) to come live in your heart.

Rueben:

Men who get loans from the bank have this fellow Jesus walking around in their hearts?

Banker:

You thinking right, Mr. Franklin. I see you the kind of man who knows how to survive in Memphis, in the world. Let me put it to you like this: As the bank president, I could see myself better trusting a Christian like myself.

Reuben:

I wouldn't object to this fellow Jesus living in my heart like he lives in your heart. But, I still don't know how to get him inside me. If he's inside you...How much room will he need?

Banker:

No room to speak of.

Reuben:

Will I have to remove anything to make room for him? Any furniture?

Banker:

I like you, Mr. Holiday. Let me minister to you, my lost brother. Open your heart to the gospel of Memphis,

Tennessee (*lifting one finger high in the air*); our gospel is one thing: money. A bible can't print itself. You can't print no bible without money. When you walked through my door, I could just smell the money on you. What I'm about to tell you is holy scripture for the business world in Memphis: we keep the money amongst those of us who have heads for business. God bless our black people, but I wonder how they get up in the morning without written instructions. I love black people, God knows I do. I've lived my whole life around them and I've yet to smell money on a single black man. Now, you can't beat them blowing a harmonica: they got the lips for it; white folk got no business blowing harmonicas. Lips too thin. If you got a floor, black people can mop it. Jesus is a rock in a weary land! (*the banker slowly transforms into a white southern Baptist preacher*). Can you see the light of Jesus, yet?

Reuben:

Not yet, but I wanna. Give me the eyes to see your Memphis gospel -

Banker:

This is the Gospel: If you got dirty dishes, black folk can wash them; if you got tarnished silver, they can polish it. If you got a mess of greens, they can cook them. Don't let no white woman mess your greens up. Get a black woman to cut/pick/wash/season and simmer your greens. Noah put a rainbow in the sky – yes he did!!! Noah put a rainbow in the sky... God (*reaching towards the floor with his own hands as if he is God)* gives every Black baby girl a green-cooking gene: collards, turnips, mustards, kale, poke salad. Ain't no greens like a colored woman's greens. Look how Jesus works – Good God Almighty! Why don't you help me lift Jesus?

Is the Holy Spirit moving in you yet, Mr. Franklin? Keep praying. Keep praying (*Reuben lowers his head and begins praying – looking up occasionally to watch the Banker preach).*

Banker:

Even the angels in heaven are pissed off because they've never tasted a black woman's greens. (*Looking towards heaven)* Holy Spirit, I think I got a convert on the line. (*Walking to Reuben and pointing to Reuben's shoes)* Look at your shoes. You got a nice pair of shoes, Mr. Holiday. Can't nobody spit-polish your leather shoes like a colored man. Do you hear me?

Reuben:

I think I see the light (*jumping to his feet)*!!!

Banker:

Jesus is the truth and the light! I refuse to let a white man shine my shoes. (*the Banker is preaching and stomping in his pulpit now).* He don't know what he's doing. Somebody help me lift Jesus? Ain't no shine like a black man's shine. In the morning, he shines. At noon, he shines. In the evening, he's shinning. Late in the midnight hour, watch him, he's shinning. Why don't you help me lift Jesus? Black men born with a shoe-shine gene. Give a black man a white rag, a tin of black polish and it's Christmas morning for him; he'd rather shine a white man's shoes than eat. He will sing, (*He puts down the plans, removes his handkerchief, which becomes his shoe-shine rag and mimics a black shoe-shine man; he dances around the Stage; he is polishing someone's shoes)* dance, move their hips (Praise the name of Jesus). They pop a shoe-shine rag (*he pops his handkerchief)* and he's God releasing a bolt of lightning. Sing one of them old Negro Spirituals. Good Lord – Jesus is a friend of mine! And before you know it, your shoes outshine the sun. Ain't Jesus a friend when you need one? (*When he finishes he is winded)* Mr. Holiday, let me share a life lesson with you: Money makes money. Let's say, I agree. I have some contractors who can read blueprints like you read the Bible. Not one word falling from my lips will return to me void, but they will accomplish every purpose for which I have sent them; Holy scripture - Jesus is a rock in a weary land! You see Jesus yet?

Reuben:

I think I'm seeing some light – yes! (*Reuben raises his hands to the sky)* Praise the Lord

Banker:

I think I got me a convert on my line! Got me a fellow believer. My people can have this plant up and producing harmonicas and pianos before you say, "The white blood of Jesus." You a new man now, Mr. Franklin. You old life is behind you. Now you walk in the newness of life. Jesus said that....

Reuben:

Everything-

Banker:

Throw off! Your old life, you old responsibilities. You're your own man now. Beholding to no man! Beholding to no woman!

Reuben:

(Beating his chest like he's King Kong) I am self-made. I knew you were the man to share this vision with me (*they both laugh).*

Banker:

(amazed with the plans and returning to his desk, he picks up the blueprints again) It's not my vision – it's the vision of Christ. It's the word of my Lord Jesus Christ that I'm sharing with you. His words have changed you, made you a different man. You no longer the same man. You are a new man in Christ Jesus, just like other white man. We need to keep this enterprise in the family. I have accountants, attorneys, electricians, painters, owners of lumber yards, framers. Now, Mr. Holiday, I'm not a racist. Jesus is my guide. My housekeeper is a black woman and her husband mows my lawn. Her daughter bakes my bread and takes care of my baby. Her son clips my hedges and clips my toenails. I love the fact they know their place and they accept their place. College is not for them. College is white-folk business. We have the skill. Where did you finish college? Yes, in New York. Your word is good enough for me: any white man's word is good enough for me. What I'm holding in my bare hands (*referencing blue prints)* – this is white folks business. Jesus is the Lily of the Valley (*the banker looks up to heaven).* After we get this thing up and running: you can hire a few black folk to sweep and mop the bathrooms, but I have

relatives who are accountants, tax people, attorneys, managers, good front-line supervisors. We are good white folk here in Memphis. Our black people polish our silver and polish our shoes cause they love this kind of simple work.

Reuben:

Sir, you are a wise man.

Banker:

I see you are not wearing a marriage band - not to get in your business. Am I sweeping too close around your front door? I have a beautiful daughter and she's single. I've been holding her back for a young man like yourself. Come by tonight for dinner: the colored lady who cooks for us was picking a mess of greens this morning. Jesus himself can't out-cook a black woman when it comes to greens.

Reuben:

I have another small issue, which a man of your statue can remedy.

Banker:

You and I are eating from the same plate, praying to the same God. Come to church on Sunday and join us: Our prayers go straight to God's ear.

Reuben:

I have some people, who may try to come in and take credit for my hard work. I have labored over these plans for years.

Banker:

I can see God's handwriting in these blue-prints. I see people like that all the time: crabs in a bucket. They latch onto a good man and try to ride his back all the way to the finish line. Don't let anyone ride your back. God is my Champion!

Reuben:

I thank you in advance for your kind attention and guidance.

Banker:

Your problem is now my problem. (*He picks up the telephone receiver and dials. Speaking into the telephone).* Hello, is this Judith? How is your husband, your children? Good to hear. Listen, we missed your family at the Cow-Tipping Jubilee last weekend: We raised a lot of money for Jesus. Yes, let me speak with the Judge. Okay. Judge, we got a new convert in my office. Yes Lord, I'm showing him the Light of Christ!!! Listen, he has a little legal problem. He designed a harmonica manufacturing plant, along with sketches for harmonicas, pianos, etc., etc., and some low-down dog is trying to steal his ideas, his birthright. Judge, you are right: the devil comes to steal, kill and destroy! Someone is trying to steal his ideas and destroy his dreams. But it won't happen to Mr. Holiday. You right, Judge, "Jesus is a friend to the friendless!."

Reuben:

You are too kind –

Banker:

He's about to start keeping company with my daughter, a great young man. College trained - up North. What can we do? Okay – sounds good to me. Do we have to be present? You can issue a TRO without us present? Judge, you are a Ram in the Bush. Okay – I see. Great. I agree with you Judge, my client will not be anyone's sacrificial lamb. He's good white folk like you and me. Good God, watch the Holy Spirit work!!! If Mr. Holiday agrees, I'm escorting him to my personal tailor: I'm buying him seven suits, seven shirts and seven pairs of shoes. My son-in-law is going to be the best dressed man walking around Memphis. (*returning the telephone to the receiver)* Mr. Holiday, Judge Block is running for reelection and he's gonna need your vote. Maybe a little folding money to line his pockets: White folks business, as I mentioned earlier. Never hurts to have a judge in your pocket, I mean, in your corner when you find yourself in a difficult legal position. (*Looking toward heaven*) Jesus is the Lion of Judah - Praise his holy name!

Reuben:

(*Removing a checkbook from his jacket pocket)* I'm writing a check for Judge Block right now (*As he writes his check, the light slowly fades).*

Act 2 Scene 4

(Light comes up in the church. There are boxes everywhere and Remmy, Will and Catherine look through the boxes, making notes.

Catherine:

We gotta lot of boxes… If I didn't know better, I'd think it was Christmas morning.

Will:

(riffling through documents) We requested documents from Floyd to review so we can prepare the Union's initial offer. We're double checking to make sure the pay rates are the same for everyone, black and white. According to class, experience, job title, responsibilities. Double checking vacation days. Verifying the number of bargaining unit members. Pulling together a seniority list.

Catherine:

(flipping through a personnel file) There are no pictures in these personnel files. But, I'm looking at these last names: Jergensen, Charleston, Callahand, Walke, Schmidt…and they are hourly employees who work on the production line

with Radio; they make almost twice as much as Radio, who has more seniority than all of them. I'm just guessing, but I don't think Schmidt is black –

Will:

Let me look at your list (*she hands him her list; he slowly looks down the list*). I can't believe this. These white men and women, according to their payroll records, are making almost double what the black employees are making. You see (*directing her to a look at a document),* this is why we need a union - to make sure all employees who are doing the same job are paid the same.

Remmy:

You sound surprised –

Will:

Uncover any more patterns like this let me know. I'm noticing white employees seem to be getting more sick days and vacation days per year, even though they have less seniority. Based on what we've discovered so far, we're need to standardize all wages, sick time and vacation time.

Remmy:

(Noticing that Catherine is lifting a heavy box) Catherine, we don't want you lifting any boxes; I promised Dennis; he threatened to peel my head like a orange if you got hurt.

Catherine:

I lifted heavier boxes at work today.

Remmy:

You point and tell us what you want; we'll hand it to you.

Catherine:

Will, thank your pastor for allowing us to use the church as our meeting place.

Remmy:

Bake him a sweet potato pie: All black preachers love sweet potato pies; that's how you know if they've been truly called to preach (*they laugh).*

Will:

We have church on Sunday, so we gotta clean this up and press Floyd for a Union office at the plant. So we can meet, strategize, plan.

Remmy:

There's a room, just off the production line. There's a water fountain just outside the door.

Catherine:

I know where you're talking about - what's in there now?

Remmy:

Mops, buckets, cleaning products, old tools. But it's a good size and we can make it work. It already has a few old file cabinets in it we can use. It's accessible to all the different departments at Ruby's. Bargaining unit members can leave their lines when they are on break, file a charge with us, and return to the line, all in a matter of minutes.

Will:

Let's send a letter to Floyd requesting it.

Catherine:

Floyd will ask for a *pound of flesh* from the union for the use of the office. We will have to give up something. What – I don't know. (*The telephone rings and Catherine answers. Floyd is on the line).* This is Catherine. Remmy and Will are here. Yes – we received the boxes of information. Thank you. We are going through the boxes now. We were just talking and we were hoping to use the room off the production line for our union office. Well, thank you, Floyd… (*placing her hand over the receiver and speaking to Will and Remmy*) Too easy; his wife must've given him some last night. *(they laugh; she speaks into the receiver again)* We can move some of the boxes in tonight. You terminated who!!!!!? (*Will and Remmy begin to gather closer to her*). When? What exactly did he do to warrant….? Okay, the union will need a copy of the rule he supposedly violated, including the date the rule was written. Also, what are the names of two women again? Sally Ruth Connor and Donna May Clark. Which shifts do these two women work? We'll need a copy of Radio's personnel file. Floyd, I don't have to tell you how this looks: the company terminates a member of the Union's negotiating team. We don't have to think about it: We will definitely file a grievance for Radio, first thing in the morning. Thanks for the call. One other thing: in preparation for Radio's grievance, we're requesting additional documents, including a copy of your investigation, notes, etc. Okay. Okay. Floyd, I understand your position, but we're filing a grievance on this one (*hanging up the telephone).* This will be the Union's first formal grievance.

Will:

What happened?

Remmy:

Floyd is just "smelling hisself."

Catherine:

Floyd is taking the position he will not give us certain documents related to Radio's termination. I need to call the Labor Board and talk to the Agent.

Remmy:

Not the same idiot Agent who we had during the election!!!

Catherine:

No, I'll ask for a different idiot. (*they laugh*)

Will:

What happened between Radio and Floyd?

Catherine:

Floyd said he gave Radio a direct order and Radio failed to follow Floyd's instruction. We'll investigate.

Remmy:

We'll get Radio's version of the facts.

Will:

(dialing the telephone). I'll call the Board Agent. (*speaking into the receiver*) This is William Dove, president of the Harmonicas & Pianos Makers Union. I need to speak with a board agent about filing some board charges. Correct... our union was recently certified. The company president just informed us he just terminated a member of our negotiation committee: his name is Rodney DuBose. I don't have the facts right now. Also, I need to file a charge alleging the company president is placing the union activities of employees under surveillance; he handed out union cards to an employee before the election....it couldn't be legal. Also, he is refusing to give us documents related to the terminated employee. Yes...the man who was terminated was the employee who Floyd gave a union card... from Floyd's very own desk. How he got the union cards only God knows. Also, we need to file another charge against Ruby's because the company's president and lead negotiator, Floyd, drafted a new rule without bargaining with the Union: We want all

charges filed on one charge and we want to name Floyd specifically in the charge. No – why would I want to first discuss this charge with the company before I file the charge? No – why would I want you to read the charge to the company before I filed the charge? The bargaining unit committee has already discussed this termination and these charges, and what I need you to do is simply complete the charge. I will drop by your office tomorrow and sign it. I am the union president – I can file a charge for the union. *(holding his hand over the receiver and talking to Catherine and Remmy)* I think we got the same idiot *(speaking in the receiver again).* As you know, we are in the middle of negotiating our 'first' labor contract; that's correct; it does look bad…Thank you. *(hangs up the telephone).*

Catherine:

Remmy, do you know Sally Ruth Connor or Donna May Clark?

Remmy:

I'll ask around.

Will:

Remmy, get the low down on these two women. Do what you do best, Honeybadger.

Remmy:

Okay.

Will:

The Union gotta come out strong. If it gets out we can't protect a member of the Union's bargaining team, we lose all respect and credibility.

Catherine:

This union will be a joke. I wouldn't pay dues to any union which can't protect its own officers. (*Light fades)*

Act 3 Scene 1

(Light comes up in Floyd's office and those present are Catherine, Remmy, and Will; they sit at one end of the table.)

Catherine:

Remmy, have you tracked down the two witnesses?

Remmy:

I got a few people working on it. Floyd supposed to turn over complete contact information for all bargaining unit members today. (*Floyd enters).*

Floyd:

(smiling; he has a small box with documents) Do I have permission to enter my own office?

Remmy:

You do.

Floyd:

(*taking a seat at the other end of the table*): I must first apologize for keeping you waiting. When you are running a music empire, your day does not belong to you – it belongs to harmonicas and pianos.

Catherine:

Floyd, you approve all disciplines issued to employees?

Floyd:

I supervise and approve all disciplines issued by Ruby's to its employees. As well as all investigations supporting our decisions to terminate.

Catherine:

Now, do you have the documents we requested to work Radio's case, including all contact information?

Floyd:

Let's discuss your request for this information. What if some of the employees did not vote in favor of the union?

Will:

The Labor Board says we get all contact information of bargaining unit members: names, addresses, and telephone numbers of every employee who voted, could have voted, or voted against the union. It's about three-hundred-and-twenty people.

Remmy:

We represent them now; every shift at Ruby's, whether or not they like the union or hate the union.

Floyd:

(becoming frustrated) How do I know the good white folks want me to pass on their home addresses and telephone numbers to the Union?

Catherine:

What?

Floyd:

These are good white folk. How do I know –

Will:

Don't matter what they want, Floyd.

Catherine:

Floyd, this standard practice. You may want to consult your attorney and ask him –

Floyd:

I don't need no attorney. You don't need to pass the Tennessee State Bar to see I'm right. In this room, right now, I'm Ruby's attorney. I don't want y'all disturbing good white folk.

Remmy:

When it comes to the union, it's not about black people or white people, men or women, we are one union.

Catherine:

What's the problem with us having this information?

Floyd:

What I want to know is how you got good white folk to vote union? What did you have on them?

Catherine:

We didn't have anything on them -

Floyd:

These are good Christian folk. Most are married; they have families. These are good white folk – not trash. They work hard. They pay their bills – on time.

Will:

We can't disclose to Ruby's anything about the inner workings of our union. Besides, Floyd, every word you just said applies to the black people who work here: We have families. We go to church. We have children, who we're raising to be good men and women. We work hard –

Floyd:

(violently sliding a file down the table to Catherine). Here's your contact information! Somehow, you tricked them to vote union…I haven't figured out how, but you did. They wouldn't get in bed with no Union; I know my people.

Catherine:

(opening the envelope and quickly checking the information, then she passes it to Remmy). Evidently not as well as you think you do. Remmy, double check this against our list (*Remmy pulls out a list and begins comparing two).* Thank you, Floyd. In addition to this information, we will need Radio's personnel file and the personnel files of other employees who were fired for the same reason you fired Radio.

Remmy:

(*not looking up, still rifling through the names and contact information*). And the personnel files of those employees, who violated the same rule Radio violated, but was neither disciplined nor terminated, including good white folk.

Floyd:

What do you mean, Remmy?

Catherine:

He means a list of every employee, for instance, who failed to follow a supervisor's direct order. And, despite this failure, he or she have received no discipline whatsoever.

Floyd:

If no discipline issued then no discipline issued. I can't create discipline out of the thin air.

Catherine:

But if their actions warranted discipline, but they received no discipline, an arbitrator will want to know their names, race, gender, and seniority dates-

Remmy:

Along with clear reasons why they weren't disciplined, while Radio was terminated for the same offense.

Floyd:

What attorney taught you that little trick?

Catherine:

We didn't land on Ellis Island last night, Floyd.

Floyd:

I'll work on assembling the information.

Will:

Let's talk about Radio. What's Ruby's official reason for firing him?

Floyd:

It's rather simple, if you can keep up: I gave him a direct order but he refused to follow my direct order. Strike number one. After he left my office, he was walking through the plant and Mrs. Sally Ruth Connor and Mrs. Donna May Clark (both good white women) reported that he "glared" at them. And he didn't smile: Strike number two and Strike three.

Will:

How does one violation become two separate charges?

Remmy:

So black men who don't smile at white women will be disciplined?

Floyd:

One strike for Mrs. Connor and one strike Mrs. May. Two people equal two violations.

Will:

Let's move forward. Which rule did he violate? Where is the rule posted and how old is the rule?

Floyd:

(sliding another envelope down the table toward the guys)
Enclosed please find in this envelope Ruby's Harmonicas & Pianos Courtesy Rule. If we don't settle this today, this will be Ruby's Exhibit Number One at the arbitration hearing. People, think long and hard before you take this to arbitration. The rule mandates we be respectful to one another, on the plant floor, in the break room, anywhere and everywhere in this facility. Given Mr. Radio chose to violate the good nature of these two women by glaring at them like a wild animal. And refusing to smile at them, I immediately drafted this new rule. His attitude problem impacts the hours, wages and conditions of employment of my employees. The good nature of these women was disturbed; they could not focus the balance of the work day; they were afraid; their work suffered; it resulted in a loss of production.

Will:

Floyd, we have already "ploughed this ground" with you: You can't run around writing new rules without bargaining with us.

Floyd:

(shaking his head in disagreement) Does not apply when we are talking about disrespecting good white folks.

Catherine:

Floyd, we'll address this new rule at the arbitration hearing. Now, do you have statements from the two women?

Floyd:

They are included here *(sliding another envelope down the table to the union)*. I have work to complete. Excuse me, I almost for something: Mr. Radio may have credibility issues. Unless you don't plan to call him to testify at his own arbitration hearing? *(Remmy, Catherine and Will listen closely)*

Catherine:

He'll testify.

Floyd:

Mr. Radio walks around Ruby's as if he pisses fourteen karat gold; he tells us he crossed Edmund Pettus Bridge in Selma on Bloody Sunday. He would have us believe he is some kind of Martin Luther King Jr. A man is measured by the truth or lies that flow from his mouth. Well, *(Floyd stands and becomes a prosecutor, pacing around the stage, giving his Closing Statement)* I did a little digging around in Selma; I shook his family tree and this is what fell out: Mr. Radio and his uncles were police and sergeants on the Selma Police Department on Bloody Sunday; he comes from a long line of head-cracking cops. Seems like Radio was swinging billy clubs, alongside his uncles. I gotta give it to him. He fooled me. He fooled you. He fooled us. He seemed like a honorable man; the sort of man whose word you could take to any bank and cash it for crisp million-dollar bills. *(Floyd laughs).* Don't feel bad. Truth is - he was cracking skulls with a billy club, along with his uncles; he wasn't carrying no bible in his hand on Bloody Sunday. Well, with this information in hand, I kept shaking his family tree, and guess what else fell out: He and his uncles took bets on Bloody Sunday. Just like the Roman Soldiers cast lots at the foot of Jesus' cross for his purple robe; but they were betting on who cracked open the most skulls. It seems his uncle, Jimmy DuBose, won the bet. He peeled fifteen to twenty skulls, like you peel bananas. *(Floyd is almost hysterical with laughter; he is "high" on this new-found knowledge).* Don't feel bad – Radio tricked me too. At one point I was gonna ask him to teach me how to piss 14 karat gold. Don't waste the union's time and money on a racist and segregationist like Radio. If you don't believe Floyd, ask him yourself. Don't take this to arbitration. Good Lord, please don't. You can't put a liar on the stand; if you do my attorney will rip him apart *(Remmy, Will and Catherine fall back in their chairs, shocked, as the light fades).*

Act 3 Scene 2

(Light comes up in the church, later the same day. Catherine, Remmy and Will are present. They review documents from a box).

Remmy:

Think Radio a liar?

Catherine:

I don't know. But it's possible to move to another State and remake yourself. He wouldn't be the first to do it.

Will:

Seems to be a good man. I can't see him swinging a billy club and cracking the skulls of Civil Rights Workers. I just can't see it; I'd hate to think I misjudge the man.

Catherine:

Just to be sure, when he stops by in a little while to discuss his case we'll ask him about Selma.

Remmy:

Is it our business? If it happened it happened a while ago… in another city… in another State. I have things in my past I don't want anyone to see. Besides, I would never walk through a door Floyd opens.

Will:

Radio is a member of our first negotiation team: We gotta give him the benefit of the doubt. We represent all three hundred-and-twenty employees: good and bad white folks; good and bad black folks; good and bad men and women. We are all stewing in the same pot.

Catherine:

At the least, we need to verify whether or not there's any truth to what Floyd is saying. (*Radio enters)*. What's up, Radio?

Remmy:

(*Remmy hands Radio an envelope)* Members of Will's church took up an offering to help pay a couple of bills, buy a few moon pies…

Radio:

(Radio is clearly worried) Thanks - every cent helps. Didn't sleep much last night.

Will:

Earlier today we had a conversation with Floyd; he gave us his version of the facts; we're just forking through what he offered. Take a seat, Radio; we need your version of what happened *(Radio sits; Remmy, Will and Catherine walk around Radio, riffling questions to Radio to rattle him)*. Floyd says one reason he fired you is you failed to follow a direct order. Let's start there. What happened?

Catherine:

Why were you in his office, alone?

Radio:

Needed to share some information with him.

Will:

Who was present during the conversation?

Radio:

Just the two of us.

Catherine:

During the conversation, were you guys interrupted by anyone: secretary? Telephone call?

Radio:

No.

Will:

How long did the conversation last?

Radio:

About a hour.

Remmy:

What did you two discuss?

Radio:

I shared with him some information I found concerning his family and Ruby's. It seems Ruby's is really the brainchild of a black woman named Ruby Holiday, an engineer and architect. Floyd's grandfather stole her idea and made millions. Ms. Holiday never saw one red cent.

Catherine:

(Remmy, Will and Catherine are astonished, and all three of them take seats around Radio). My God!!! How did Floyd respond to that stone in his shoe?

Radio:

He refused to hear the truth: His Gold Mile is a mile-long lie. His grandfather never finished college; Ms. Holiday and her family reached out to him when he landed in Memphis, gave him a job, made him a man, and he repaid them by stealing her plans, blue-prints. From what I managed to piece together, Ms. Holiday and Floyd's grandfather were supposed to get married; they definitely had some kind of relationship.

Remmy:

I know Floyd turned beet-red –

Radio:

He offered me money to keep quiet. I told Floyd truth ain't got no price tag. He needs to do right by Ms. Holiday's children, grandchildren.

Will:

If you're Floyd, everyone has a price. During the conversation did he give you a direct order?

Radio:

He asked for a package I had with me.

Catherine:

What package?

Radio:

Some research information -

Remmy:

Did it have anything to do with your job on the production line?

Radio:

Nothing whatsoever.

Will:

Did Floyd see the contents of the package?

Radio:

No. The package was the property of the Memphis Public Library; it's an unpublished autobiography of Ms. Holiday; the only copy to my knowledge; I had to promise, on my life, I'd take good care or it. I've already returned it to the library.

Remmy:

This is why I would never walk through a door that Floyd opens… I knew this was some foolishness!!!! One issue down and two to go.

Catherine:

Radio, focusing on the time after your conversation with Floyd, did you have a misunderstanding with anyone?

Radio:

I was off work. So after I met with Floyd, I walked the Gold Mile, again; then I walked along the production area, picked up my dirty uniforms, and then I left the plant.

Catherine:

Wait…On the day you and Floyd spoke in his office, you were not clocked-in?

Radio:

Exactly – that was my off day.

Remmy:

Floyd can't discipline an employee who is not at work.

Will:

Okay. Okay. Let's stay focused. While you were walking around the facility to pick up your uniforms, did you have any conversation with anyone?

Floyd:

Not that I recall.

Will:

Let's try this a different way. Do you know anyone by the names of …Remmy, what were those names again?

Remmy:

Sally Ruth Connor and Donna May Clark.

Radio:

Nope.

Catherine:

Did you have any conversations with any white women?

Radio:

Nope.

Remmy:

Did you stare at two white females? Did you frown at any –

Catherine:

Did you walk past any white women and fail to speak, fail to smile –

Radio:

Wait a minute! (*Raising his voice in anger)* I don't have to smile at nobody if I don't want to. Nobody owns me. I work at Ruby's but Ruby don't own me. White folk can't tell me when to smile, how long to smile, where to smile, who to smile at.

Remmy:

Radio is right: He don't have to smile at anyone. This is crazy. (*pointing at Radio)*This man's whole livelihood is in jeopardy because Floyd won't face the fact his grandfather maybe a thief, and Floyd has been living a lie his whole life.

Catherine:

(Standing and walking around like she's an attorney, planning her next move) Floyd will need to clear his calendar for this, as soon as possible. Let's plan to meet with him tomorrow. We'll need to review the rest of these documents and get ready for the meeting. Off the bat, Floyd needs to understand we're fighting Radio's termination, all the way to the supreme court.

Remmy:

Radio needs his job back; he has bills like we all have bills. Catherine, what you're planning could take a lot of time. If we don't wanna drag this thing out with a trial, we gotta give Floyd something to get Radio's job back.

Will:

Like what?

Remmy:

Offer to withdraw our pending Labor Board charges, if he reinstates Radio. Floyd hates bad publicity like he loves money. Ruby's breaking ground for a new plant in Nashville.

Will:

I see where you going, and Floyd has been on cloud nine since he got those government contracts –

Catherine:

But he has to keep his nose clean: No labor unrest, No strikes, no labor board charges, no leaks to the press. The last thing he needs is the Union writing a letter to each branch of the service, and disclose Floyd is terminating employees who are members of the Union's negotiating team –

Radio:

While we're in the middle of negotiating our first labor contract.

Catherine:

Let's write seven letters and have them in hand tomorrow when we meet with him.

Radio:

Floyd will piss in his pants if he thinks there's any chance he will lose those federal contracts. Not to mention what impact this could have on that groundbreaking in Nashville.

Will:

And his plans to import Ruby's pianos outside the borders of the country.

Catherine:

(Walking toward the telephone). I'll call the Board and have those idiots at the Board file more labor charges. I would clue the Board into what's happening, but they would probably screw it up. Radio, while I'm talking to the Board, Remmy and Will have a few more questions for you.

Remmy:

Floyd's attorney will ask you certain questions to shake you up. If you make any mistake the judge will probably not believe you, and rule in Ruby's favor, not giving you your job back.

Radio:

What is it?

Remmy:

According to Floyd, who did a little investigation of your family's history, your uncles were Selma Police Officers on Bloody Sunday March.

Will:

Is DuBose a common name around Selma? Maybe Floyd just got his facts wrong.

Radio:

I had three uncles who were Selma Police (*Will and Remmy look surprised*); very light-skinned. Even voted before other black folk.

Will:

Really? How was that possible?

Radio:

Easy. They passed. I have two uncles with eyes bluer than any white man's eyes. The other had green eyes – looked just like a snake; some said he'd hypnotize you if you looked into his eyes. I never looked into his eyes; grand momma said she accidentally stepped over a snake when she was pregnant with him. So, how the fact that my uncles were police have anything to do with me?

Remmy:

On Bloody Sunday, did they take-off work?

Radio:

Listen, I'm not proud of the fact that my uncles were blocking the way of the Civil Rights Workers on Bloody Sunday, but I ain't gone deny them; family is family.

Remmy:

According to Floyd, you've told people at the plant you marched with the Civil Rights Workers on that day. Is that true?

Radio:

I never broadcasted I marched, but if it came up in discussion, I would tell people what happened.

Remmy:

Floyd says you were actually a Selma Police Officer and you hurt a lot of people.

Radio:

I never worked as a Selma police officer, only my uncles. The day before the march, my uncles begged me not to march; they warned me they couldn't protect me. I told them not to worry about me – I was marching. They said if I wanted to vote they could make it happen. I told them it ain't just about me; everybody, black and white and Chinese and Indian – everybody got the right to get a ballot and vote their choice. Told my uncle that all men and women born in this country gotta right to vote.

Will:

(*becoming exasperated*) Radio, let's get down to business: you want us to believe your own uncles beat you?

Radio:

You ever marched? (*Remmy and Will shake their heads no).* You're lucky if you only got your head bust open like a watermelon. (*Catherine returns to the conversation, having completed her telephone call to the Board agent).* On Bloody Sunday, we're marching on the sidewalk, crossing Edmund Pettus Bridge. Two by two like we marching into Noah's Ark. Except we marching for the Right to Vote: two-by-two, shoulder to shoulder, walking into Noah's Ark. Not hurting anyone (*standing and walking stage Left; a slowly, slowly light narrows on Radio, over the course of his explanation, so the audience focuses on his story. Radio is back on the bridge)*. Bloody Sunday wasn't the first time we'd crossed that bridge: We'd crossed the bridge to clean white folks' houses; to take care of their children; to sweep and mop their floors; to cook their food. But this day, we're carrying our Bibles - no swords - no shields. Naw – naw - My bible is my sword and shield that day. We're not wearing protective gear, unless you talking about the head scarves the women wearing or the hankerchiefs us men had in our back pockets; unless you talking about the thin coats the men wearing, or the cotton sweaters the women wearing. We're not wearing gas masks. Why would we need gas masks? We got our Bibles. Two by two, marching into the Noah's Ark. We don't have no respirators, unless you talking about the hats we are wearing or the pocketbooks the women are carrying. We don't need no respirators cause we have our Bibles.

Well, we slowly top the incline in the middle of the bridge. We see the police at the foot of the bridge, holding night sticks; those barking dogs – ready to tear into us. Then, State Troopers shoot tear gas canisters "at us." Not into the air, not over our heads. Everybody know you shoot tear gas toward the ground, not directly at our heads. All the police shooting tear gas cartridges like they shooting a shotgun, like they hunting rabbits. And we're the rabbits! No, we're not rabbits cause we carrying our Bibles and rabbits don't read God's word. Rabbits don't march for the right to vote. Right? I know the constitution don't allow rabbits to vote – right! I don't know: Maybe if we rabbits or cats or dogs, maybe then we could vote. Naw – but we black men and women and white men and women marching for the Right to get black people to vote, just like white people vote; marching to the Alabama State Capital for the right to simply mark "yes" or "no" on a ballot; a ballot ain't nothing but a piece of paper that cost less than a piece of penny candy. Tear Gas canisters falling out of the sky like manna from heaven. My God! My God! - don't they see we got women walking alongside us shoulder to should, joined at the hip. It's hard to see because of the clouds of tear gas. Everything is a thick fog. I can't see my feet; the gas burns my eyes and burns my nose. I'm sneezing, coughing up my guts. I cover my nose and mouth with my hankerchief; then with my hat, but that don't stop the burning. I can't stop coughing cause I inhale tear gas into my lungs every time I open my mouth. People are coughing, vomiting. Now policemen crawling over us like ants. I make-out one of the marchers, a young black girl from Spelman marching with us; the police beating her with billy clubs like she's a drum. She's screaming, (*Radio screams*), "We got the victory! We got the victory in Christ!" But these police don't care nothing about Jesus, let alone his cross. So, I am running toward her and I begin throwing the police off her and just when I manage to cover her, they begin drumming on my back with billy clubs; now my back is a drum, but young Spelman is okay (*the light slowly brightens and Radio begins to return to his chair; Radio is a heavy weight boxer walking back to his corner after 7 hard rounds*). Yes Sir, we paid the cost for the ferry that day, trying to cross Edmund Pettus Bridge. And the ferryman was picky that day; he wouldn't take one red penny, only human blood and broken bones (*light fades*).

Act 3 Scene 3

(Light comes up on Floyd in his office, sipping a cup of coffee. There's a knock at the door that startles Floyd).

Floyd:

Come in. (*Enter Will, Catherine, Remmy and Radio. Floyd is surprised to see Radio).* The Union is here - top of the morning to you. (*Remmy, Will, and Catherine sit in the chairs in front of Floyd's desk, but Radio stands throughout this final Scene, moving around, as imposing as the Truth is imposing and uncompromising).*

Will:

Before we get started, Floyd, I want to make sure we're all on the same page: if we reach an agreement (verbally or in writing), it is binding on Ruby's?

Floyd:

Agreed.

Catherine:

Let's move to the table behind us. We need to spread out some documents so we can talk?

Floyd:

Of course – my office is your castle. (*They begin to move toward the table. Floyd is at the end of the table and the others are near the other end of the table. Radio walks about the office, looking at photos on Floyd's desk; sometimes he stands behind each of the union representatives. You can tell this begins to unnerve Floyd. Truth is always imposing and always makes some people uncomfortable).*

Catherine:

Floyd, thank you providing us some the documents we asked for.

Will:

We can see it required a lot of work and time.

Floyd:

The Union asks and Ruby provides.

Catherine:

We're placing our cards on this table. We will share with you how we plan to use the documents you gave us, during the arbitration hearing. Maybe we can settle this and get contracts negotiations back on track.

Will:

We reviewed Ruby's records and saw quite a few irregularities, when comparing the treatment black employees received when compared to the treatment white employees received.

Floyd:

Irregularities? Ruby's is not aware of any such irregularities -

Remmy:

Floyd, you agree if two employees violate the same rule they should be issued the same discipline, all things being equal?

Floyd:

Ruby's is fair, always been above-board.

Will:

You say Radio refused to follow your direct order?

Floyd:

Yes and I clearly told him it was a "direct order;" I'm ready and willing to place my hand on my mother's bible and so testify. Radio?

Radio:

(walking around the office): You said it was a direct order.

Floyd:

There you have it: Radio's admission sustains his termination. Ain't God Good!?

Remmy:

No. No. No. *(Remmy raises one hand)* Pump your brakes, Floyd, we're just beginning.

Will:

Reviewing Ruby's personnel files, *(pulling out Margaret Anderson's disciplinary letter),* there is this case of Margaret Anderson. Are you aware of her case?

Floyd:

I approve all disciplinary actions at Ruby's. You should find my initials at the bottom of each document.

Will:

It seems Anderson works in the same production department as Radio. You issued her a letter of warning, because "you" gave her a direct order to repaint a piano; the customer was the Fitzgerald Opera House in Little Rock; you told her the color had not met the customer's color requirement. But, she refuses to repaint the piano and signs the Order, releasing the shipment of a $15,000 piano to Little Rock. The customer refused shipment; the piano shipped back to Ruby's – at Ruby's expense; it was repainted and shipped back to Little Rock. Ruby's ate all shipping costs. According to this letter of warning, despite these additional costs, Anderson only received a verbal counseling, not even a written discipline. She's still employed at Ruby's, doing the same job (*Will hands Anderson's personnel file to Floyd, who begins to thumb through the file)* If she had followed your direct order, Ruby would not have lost hundreds of dollars on the deal. Right?

Floyd:

Yes. But, I know Ms. Anderson. She simply exercised her discretion here. She's good white folk. She's married, with children. Her husband's my mechanic.

Catherine:

Floyd, at Radio's termination hearing, the judge will compare these disciplines and wonder why you only issued a verbal discipline to Anderson, who costs Ruby's hundreds of dollars, but you terminated Radio? Unlike Anderson, Radio did not cost Ruby one thin dime. If anyone should have been terminated, she should have been terminated; or, at the least, suspended for a few days. The judge will see Ruby seems to give special treatment to Anderson; this evidence will win our case; these are your own personnel files.

Floyd:

(folding his arms across his chest in defiance) We'll have to disagree on this comparable. Like I said, she's a good Christian woman; she did not walk into my office and ask for a union card; she never signed a union card -

Remmy:

Floyd, you're making this too easy. You can't give special treatment to people who did not sign union cards. And how you know she didn't sign a union card is another labor board violation we don't wanna get into right now.

Floyd:

What I just said was off the record…..

Catherine:

We have another comparable: Blake Winters, a probationary employee who still works in the packaging department. (*Opening the personnel file of Blake and withdrawing his disciplinary form)* He came to work, seemingly having drunk too much liquor the night before, according to your supervisor's report in this disciplinary record. Seems his supervisor, having inspected a $10,000 piano for Morehouse College in Atlanta, gave Blake a direct order. He ordered Blake to add more padding, because both the piano's sustaining pedal and loud pedal could be damaged in transport, as well as the key bed. Blake ignored the direct order, and the piano was improperly padded for transport. Blake, who is noticeably drunk, cursed his supervisor, and signed the Order, releasing the product for shipment. When the piano had arrived at Morehouse, not only were a few keys damaged on the key bed, but many of the soft and loud pedals were totally destroyed. Morehouse retained a local company to make the necessary repairs and sent Ruby's a bill (*holding up the document and waiving it in the air).* Floyd, this was another significant loss. Blake is also white employee.

Remmy:

Had Blake followed his supervisor's direct order and added more cushion, chances are Ruby's could have realized a better profit on the piano.

Radio:

And Blake was not even disciplined for being drunk. Was he?

Catherine:

We double checked Blake's file and he was not disciplined for being drunk, at work. I don't like to see anyone lose his or her job, but you should have issued some level of discipline to Blake.

Will:

As a probationary employee, you could have fired him – on the spot.

Floyd:

Hand that to me (*Floyd thumbs through the file).* Maybe his discipline fell out as we were ferrying the documents to you.

Besides, I know Blake. Yes, he has a little drinking problem but his daddy has a drinking problem and his daddy before him. But, Blake is trying to turn his life around. He's a family man and he and his wife have three beautiful daughters, two dogs and two cats. If I'd terminated Blake, how would he pay his mortgage each month? Who would put food on his table…have a heart?

Remmy:

Like Anderson, the judge will see Blake got more favorable treatment when compared to Radio. Radio has more seniority, and he's a top producer; he has no previous discipline. Blake was probationary. Finally, Radio didn't cost Ruby one penny by not handing you that package.

Radio:

Information not related to my work at Ruby's.

Floyd:

Blake could be my son – he's good white folk too.

Catherine:

These two examples are just the tip of the mountain, Floyd. Once you turn over the other documents we've requested, we'll introduce twenty-five or more comparable situations where white employees seemingly received some sort of special treatment.

Remmy:

(*speaking to Will*) Show Floyd that ace we've been holding.

Will:

Floyd, this Radio's time card (*Holding up a Time Card)*, the day you and Radio met in your office, correct?

Floyd:

Let me see that. I'm not taking the position that the Union created this document, but I have to be sure. (*Will hands Floyd the time card)* This ain't my first rodeo... Okay. *(Oddly, then Floyd sniffs the time card)*. This looks like an official Ruby document.

Catherine:

Floyd, you gave us that time card…

Will:

That Time Card you holding shows Radio was off work when he had met with you that day...in this very office. He came in on his own time, Floyd.

Floyd:

This has got to be a mistake. (*After Floyd reads the document, he leans back in his seat and laughs, realizing his plan has failed).* Well, well, well... Mr. Radio, Mr. Martin Luther King Jr., Mr. Civil Rights Leader, Mr. Voting Rights.

Radio:

My name's Radio. (*spelling his name very slowly, like he's talking to a child)* R-a-d-i-o.

Catherine:

Floyd, you can't discipline an employee for a work-related offense when the employee is not clocked-in. It's not even a stretch for a reasonable judge to see Radio was probably terminated because he's a union member and because he serves on the Union's negotiating team.

Remmy:

Not because he refused to follow your direct order.

Will:

Not to mention the EEOC would love to get their hands on these personnel records, which show you give special treatment to white employees.

Radio:

Floyd, don't pick up a hornet's nest and not expect to get stung.

Floyd:

Radio ain't the name on your birth certificate. Why'd someone name their baby Radio? You standing here, flat-footed, in my office and verbally falsifying your birth certificate. I could fire you for verbally altering an official governmental document. Can't I, Catherine? Remmy? Will? (*the three shake their heads in disbelief*).

Radio:

How would you know what's on my birth certificate?

Floyd:

(*rising from his chair, irritated)* Mr. Selma, Alabama. Maybe you've slipped through Ruby's fingers on the insubordination charge, but not the Courtesy Rule Violation.

Catherine:

Floyd, don't add a verbal threat charge on top of everything else. For once in your life – (*Floyd takes his seat again)*. As for a Courtesy Rule… no one seated here ever read any Courtesy Rule. Not even Will who has worked here since he was sixteen years old. Have you, Will?

Will:

Not since the first day I walked through Ruby's front door. Floyd, what's really going on?

Floyd:

Will, I finally got Mr. Martin Luther King Jr. dead to right on my Courtesy Rule Violation. This snake can't wiggle out of this one. Now (*pointing at Radio with his index finger*)who has picked up a hornet's nest not expecting to get stung, Mr. R-a-d-i-o.

Remmy:

Tell us about this courtesy rule which has been around since Ruby's foundation was laid.

Floyd:

(He stands and becomes a white southern Baptist preacher, roaming about the Stage, on occasion, coming into close contact with Radio). On the date in question, Mr. Martin Luther King Jr. here walks past two employees, who were on the clock, and looked at them in a threatening way, placing these good white women in a dangerous predicament; the two became flustered and had trouble working the rest of their shifts…a clear violation of our Courtesy Rule.

Radio:

I didn't stare at anyone -

Floyd:

You calling these two white women liars!? Why would they lie on you? They saw you with their own eyes – they were clearly flustered. Couldn't concentrate the rest of the day. You telling me you didn't walk on the production floor when you left my office?

Radio:

I did.

Floyd:

So, you admit you flustered these women when you stared at them, costing Ruby's dollars in down production time?

Radio:

No, I'm admitting I walk through the production area toward the lockers so I could get my dirty uniforms. I don't know these two women you're talking about -

Floyd:

But, you admit prowling –

Radio:

I ain't no animal! I'm a man. I don't prowl – I can't control what white women "think" when they see me.

Remmy:

Floyd, he can't control what these women –

Floyd:

I say we let a judge make this call. Let him decide who to believe: Dr. Martin Luther King Jr. or some good white folk.

Will:

Floyd, this is not going anywhere …there are only twenty four hours in a day.

Catherine:

Floyd, if this goes to hearing, you will put your witnesses and the stand and so will we. But, I don't think you want to go to a hearing – not on this one.

Floyd:

You ain't figuring on letting Radio testify?!

Radio:

Why not – the judge needs to hear the truth –

Floyd:

You wouldn't know the truth if it knocked on your front door and asked for a cup of coffee. Jesus!

Catherine:

(pulling out the seven letters and waving them in the air. As she discusses the contents of each letter, she drops them on the table in front of Floyd): Floyd, what I'm holding in my hand are seven letters, addressed, stamped, and ready to mail. Letter number one includes affidavits from the two women who rebut your allegation Radio glared at them and/or refused to smile; these good white women will testify; if we don't settle this today, they will also testify you verbally threatened them with termination if they did not sign the erroneous statements that you drafted. Letter number two is addressed to the United States Teamsters Transportation Union, whose members operate the eighteen-wheelers which transports raw goods to Ruby's and move Ruby's finished products across the country; they're a loyal union to their brother and sister unions. I can simply drop them this note concerning the status of our negotiations, including the fact you have terminated a member of the bargaining committee.

Remmy:

And include the fact that you have several charges pending before the Labor Board. Only God knows what the country's largest transportation union will do?

Catherine:

Letters three through six are to the Contract Specialists for the Army, Navy, and Marines, informing them of the current labor unrest at Ruby's; You wouldn't want to lose those contracts, Floyd.

Then, there is this final letter, number seven. I would prefer to send letter number seven and I promise to send this letter, if we settle this today. This letter is to the Labor Board, withdrawing the Union's pending charges against Ruby's, if you reinstate Radio with back-pay; rescind the Courtesy Rule and all other rules you've unlawfully implemented since Ruby's employees voted union.

Will:

Floyd, you will also agree to stop threatening employees, forcing them to lie; and stop asking employees about how they feel about the union and why they voted for the Union.

Catherine:

You will also begin negotiating with us, immediately, for a labor contract. (*Holding up what looks like a 30-page document)* Floyd, this is the Union's 30-page initial proposal for a labor contract (*she hands it to Radio who takes it to Floyd; Floyd accepts the proposal)*.

Floyd:

(screaming at Radio) Ruby's employees should know the blood on your hands from Bloody Sunday wasn't your own blood: it was the blood of college students, preachers, teachers. Real heroes! Why don't you tell the truth? You ain't nobody's Savior!! You ain't nobody's Jesus!!

Radio:

(becoming angry, approaching Floyd, but the group intercedes between the two men) Never claimed to be anybody's Savior. Nothing special about me: I'm just an ordinary man, Floyd.

Floyd:

But you want us to believe you piss 14 karat gold.

Radio:

Can't control what other people believe or think. What they drink or what they piss. Floyd, you don't know nothing about what happened cause you weren't on "that" bridge on "that" day in Selma…were you?

Floyd:

You're fake as a seven-dollar bill!!!!! But, I must confess: you even had me fooled. Had everyone at Ruby's fooled. (*acting as if he is shaking a tree)* But I shook, shook, shook your Selma family tree and a lot of lies fell into my hands. You ain't nobody's Martin Luther King Jr. You didn't carry no bible on that bridge; if you carried anything it was a night stick.

Radio:

If I'm a fraud, then so are you, your father, and your grandfather. This ain't about me and you know it: It's about the lie your family been sleeping with and living all these years. Lies resulting in a fat back account for you and your family. Lies that built this plant and buttered your bread.

Floyd:

My grandfather was an industrial prophet -

Radio:

Floyd, your grandfather brushed his teeth with lies. And so do you, every day you don't own the truth.

Floyd:

He was a man of integrity and grit - *(looking up to heaven)* a visionary –

Radio:

He was a seven-dollar bill!

Floyd:

(*Addressing everyone but Radio)* Don't listen to Radio. His tongue is forked. Grand-daddy was a man who landed on Ellis Island, with only a dented harmonica and a dream. He worked hard to create all this -

Radio:

He landed on Ellis Island with a milk jug - that's it. Nothing else. No harmonica, dented or otherwise.

Floyd:

Because of his dream, you got money in your pocket, bread on your table, gas in your car, money in the bank, clothes on your back –

Radio:

No – I work five days a week, sometimes six days a week. Even if my white coworkers, with less seniority, make more than I do. I work and take care of my family.

Floyd:

Every crumb on your table is there because of my family.

Radio:

Floyd, listen -

Floyd:

You act like you from money. Like you leave $20 tips on the table. You some kind of Nubian King? No!

Radio:

I may not be a King, but I don't ignore the truth. Especially if someone is spoon-feeding -

Floyd:

Truth! (*Sniffing the air).* You smell like a lie. Fake –

Radio:

I'm no fraud! Floyd, what kind of lie is this…) (*Radio rips off his shirt and buttons fly everywhere and then turns his back to Floyd, Remmy, Will, and Catherine. Floyd, seeing Radio's back, covers his mouth with his hand and falls back into his chair like he's been shot. Keloid scars criss-cross Radio's back; it looks like a Keloid tree. Catherine looks away, Remmy and Will shake their heads, and Will then drops his head).* Is this tree on my back fake?!!! When you were shaking my family tree in Selma did any fruit from "this" tree fall into your hands!? Floyd?

Floyd:

(*For the first time in the play, Floyd is humble).* I'm sorry. Radio. My God, I'm sorry…. Catherine, let's send letter number seven; we'll work this out. Radio, you can come back to work first thing Monday.

Catherine:

Floyd, *(handing him the letter)* the letter is already stamped:
I'll trust you will drop it in the mail, today.

Floyd:

I'll drive it to the post office - myself (*light slowly fades)*.

The End

The End

About the Author

Multi-talented, Gregory Powell, is a true Renaissance Man. Besides being a playwright and poet, he is a lawyer, and educator and minister of the Gospel, who worked for several years as a journalist. In the legal field, he has worked as a labor and employment law attorney for the federal government almost twenty years and operates his own labor and employment law consulting firm. He also currently works as Professor of Ethics and Leadership Development at William Seymour College.

Gregory graduated from Morehouse College with a BA in journalism. He earned his Doctor of Laws Degree from the University of Wisconsin-Madison Law School, a Master of Fine Arts Degree in Creative Writing from the University of Alabama-Tuscaloosa, and a Master of Divinity from the School of Divinity at Regent University.

Previously, his poetry has been published in *Callaloo, African American Review, Langston Hughes Review, Arkansas Review, story south (on-line journal), Antietam Review, Poem, touchstone, Mosaic,* and *Lake Effect* and *Tar Wolf Review.* His first poetry collection, *Tin Ears,* published under the Broad Wing imprint of Seymour Press in 2017 was nominated for a Pulitzer Prize.

Gregory can be reached at **gpowell65@gmail.com** or though Seymour Press at **Seymourpress.org.**

www.ingramcontent.com/pod-product-compliance
Lightning Source LLC
La Vergne TN
LVHW080330110826
845155LV00024B/141